HOW TO PROSPER IN THE COMING APOCALYPSE

by Richard Curtis
with illustrations by Michael C. Witte

ST. MARTIN'S PRESS
NEW YORK

10 9 8 7 6 5 4 3 2 1

First Edition

Library of Congress Cataloging in Publication Data

Curtis, Richard.
  How to prosper in the coming apocalypse.

  1. Disaster--Anecdotes, facetiae, satire, etc.
I. Title.
PN6231.D657C87   818'.5407   80-23213
ISBN 0-312-39611-2 (pbk.)

For Leslie, who makes me laugh

Disclaimer

This book represents the author's opinions only. If the reader disagrees with them, he is free to take the book and jam it in his ear. It is sold with the understanding that the author is not attempting to render legal, financial, or similar services, but rather is strictly engaged in manipulating the anxieties of the insecure and feeding the fantasies of the avaricious. If the reader desires legal, financial, or other expert advice, he should seek the services of a professional. My son Lester just hung up his shingle and will give you a good price.

Acknowledgments

My gratitude to Ashton Applewhite, my editor, whose idea put the spark to the tinder; to my brother David, Robert Twombly, and Judy Negron for an evening of inspired if slightly sick ideas; to my sister Debbie for one inspired and *very* sick idea; to Al Hart, who'll do anything to get his name into an acknowledgment; and to Leslie Tonner, who touched every page with her magic wand.

Contents

A Word About My Newsletter

Throughout this book I refer frequently to my monthly newsletter, *Apocalypse Soon*. However, I don't wish to give the impression that I am soliciting subscriptions. True, because my family writes, lays out, prints, collates, staples, and mails the newsletter at $200 per subscription, it's almost like minting money. But the reader should not feel the newsletter is vital to understanding this book. Of course, I have omitted from these pages certain formulas, charts, graphs, and statistics which may be found only in the newsletter and without which the reader may make some rather serious errors of judgment. But be assured you will not go to prison because of these omissions, or if you do it won't be for more than three to five years if you behave yourself.

Apocalypse Soon started as a series of anonymous letters to the manager of my bank threatening him and his family with mutilation if he didn't stop hiring ethnic minority members. After the FBI visited me, I toned these down and began expanding on them until they embraced the full spectrum of human endeavor. I am now capable of pontificating on finance, politics, sex, religion, the arts, and sports, and of speaking intelligently on medieval illuminated manuscripts, Russian ballet, and phallic imagery in *Don Quixote*. Go ahead, ask me about those windmills!

Foreword

Let's face it, my friend, the end of the world is nigh. Where are you going to be when it staggers, totters, and collapses? Underneath the rubble as usual, Schmucko? Or are you going to wise up at last and live out the end in high style?

This is the book that tells you how you can strike it rich while your neighbors, friends, and in-laws are going to hell in a handbasket, the book that will enable you to watch the final convulsions from a well-stuffed rocker on the veranda of your country estate. While all around you are losing their heads in the imminent conflagration, you can be gearing up for windfall profits that will make the oil companies look like mama-and-papa candy stores.

The author, whose last three books *(You Can Profit from the Vietnamese War, Cash in on Cambodia's Wretched Masses,* and *I Tripled My Income During the Takeover of the Grand Mosque)* accurately predicted profitable opportunities in the miseries of small numbers of people, now tackles the twilight of humanity in one comprehensive volume that not only touches on every aspect of the decline of civilization, but whose high list price will rake in a king's ransom in royalties and swell his Swiss account to almost unmanageable proportions.

This book is organized in such a way that, starting with the first page you come to and turning each page consecutively until you get to the last one and reading all the words on each page, you will have completed it. In the course of which the following questions will be answered:

What does that funny little © on the copyright page mean?

Precisely when is the world scheduled to end, and will there be enough sanitation men to clean up afterwards?

Will a six-month Treasury bill paying 14 percent interest yield more than half an hour of looting at Fortunoff's department store?

In a prolonged siege of your hoarded food by your neighbors, is it better to fire your semiautomatic at them in short bursts or to empty the clip in one long one?

Why is a meal consisting of Oreo cookies, Velveeta, and Courvoisier VSOP the best survival diet known to nutritionists?

What is the most efficient way to stockpile toilet paper: end up, or on its side?

Who holds the Guinness record for most margins responding to a margin call?

Who said, "Every man over forty is a scoundrel"? It's got nothing to do with this book, but it's been bothering me all night.

What kind of interest can you get at a sperm bank? Is there a penalty for early withdrawal?

Do welfare rolls come with butter, or is it extra?

Are wage-price controls as counterinflationary as, say, slavery?

In a rapidly falling bond market, which is easier to liquidate: your municipals or your broker?

Why is there a thriving black market in prune yogurt?

Why are your Social Security payments going to support a bunch of old people?

Does the President have the right to confiscate your Ritz Crackers during a national emergency? To nationalize Wendy's? To conscribe women for the Food and Drug Administration softball team?

Is it sound fiscal policy to put the firstborn of every family to the sword?

Is a Meissen figurine a more desirable collectible than a Remington 870 12-gauge riot gun with 2500 rounds of ammo?

Does the coming collapse of the capitalist system mean no more Baskin-Robbins Rocky Road?

What Is an Apocalypse, and Why Can't People Just Call It Doomsday?

"Assessing your personal megadeath potential is simple using this handy map."
—GAR SMITH, *New West* magazine

The most important things for you to concern yourself with in the coming bad years is, Who's responsible and how can I get even? It is essential that we find someone to blame and really beat the hell out of him. Sure, the tragedy of the past is that we are condemned to repeat it, but does that make you feel any better? No! Your first task is to find a scapegoat.

It will be recalled that Germany in the 1930s blamed the Jews for its economic woes. Jews are good scapegoats because with their long pointy tails they are easily visible, but they are definitely not to blame for the present recession. True, one memorable bar mitzvah did wreck the economy of Scarsdale in the summer of 1976, but Scarsdale's economy had been shaky for some time anyway, what with the inordinate amount of money the town had spent on wall-to-wall carpeting for its sewer system.

Modern Americans are fortunate in having many scapegoats to blame: the Arabs for their oil pricing, the Russians for the arms race, the Japanese for their exports, the Federal Reserve, the bankers, welfare recipients, stockbrokers, Republicans, Democrats, the President, the Governor, the Mayor. Our common sense, however, tells us that none of these can accurately be cited as the source of America's financial doldrums.

That is because the true source of America's financal doldrums is the old American Basketball Association. This nation was doing just fine until the merger of the A.B.A. with the National Basketball

1

Association. Our national debt just prior to the merger was a manageable five hundred billion dollars; only ten million people were out of work; and only fifteen million more people on welfare drained the nation's lifeblood; murder, rape, burglary, larceny, arson, and vandalism caused untold suffering to no more than one person in every three households.

But observe the astonishing change on the very day the A.B.A. and N.B.A. inked their pact: the balance of world geopolitics was violently and permanently altered, social unrest escalated at an unprecedented rate, and international recessionary trends manifested themselves with unwonted ferocity. Plus, it rained like hell that day—flooded subways, battered umbrellas, not a taxi to be had for love or money! What a mess!

It should be particularly noted that on that day, the cost of garbanzo beans registered an incredible 8.9 fluctuation on the Kremnitzer-Fergenmacher scale. Because garbanzos are vital to the production of reinforced pantyhose, they are traditionally used by social scientists as the most sensitive and accurate barometer of economic change. A mere three-ounce fluctuation in any given month has proven time and again to be a harbinger of good times or bad, and on A.B.A.-N.B.A. merger day you couldn't find a single can on the shelf of the A&P on Madison Avenue and Eighty-seventh Street. The very next week you had the Great Pantyhose Scare.

Note, too, the significant dip in sales of long-playing polka albums, virtually a mirror image of the growth in pro basketball salaries. Goddamn things fell right off the chart!

So I say, let's get these basketball players and hurt them bad. Break their fingers! Smash their kneecaps! Now, you say that punishing basketball players won't bring back a stable economy. Not true! In February 1978, when pro basketball was suspended for three days to allow for conversion of player heights to the metric system, the Dow Jones average soared, consumer prices leveled out for the first time since the McKinley assassination, and put-and-call volume on the Chicago sowbelly exchange hit a peak unmatched before or since. Actually, there weren't that many puts, but the calls! "Sowbellies! Sowbellies!" You couldn't cross Michigan Avenue without hearing some damn fool hollering, "Sowbellies!"

The Apocalypse and You

Now that we have determined how we got to this sorry pass and have avenged ourselves with the blood of the transgressors, we must turn our attention to the coming apocalypse and ask ourselves this critical question: which end of the tube do you want to be on when the world starts going down it?

In order to answer, it is essential for you to recognize whether or not you have an apocalyptic personality—whether, to use the scientific term, you have "apocalybility." In his landmark study conducted at the University of California's Cahuenga campus, pathologist Yitzik Marylebone measured volunteers' responses to what he called doomsday stimuli, of which there are five known, three inferable from evidence, and a couple more awaiting matching grants from the Corporation for Public Broadcasting.

Among Marylebone's tests for apocalybility are the following:

1. Do you flinch when a meteorite is hurtling toward your face?

2. Are you afraid to rabbit-chop your mother in the throat when she tries to cadge your emergency rations?

3. If a ten-day bank holiday were declared tomorrow, would you cancel your dentist appointment?

4. Does the prospect of a protracted and exquisitely agonizing death from radiation poisoning bother you?

5. Which do you think it's nobler in the mind to do: suffer the slings and arrows of outrageous fortune? Or take arms against a sea of troubles and by opposing end them?

Marylebone supplemented this test with a questionnaire which included the following questions:

4

DEVELOPING THE SURVIVALIST MENTALITY
Don't be afraid to rabbit-chop your mother if she tries
to cadge your emergency rations.

True or False?

1. There is no relationship between plummeting bond yields and battered wives.

2. Mussolini came to power after mass sitdown strikes by standup comics.

3. Sixty-five percent of your Social Security contribution goes toward reparations to the Confederacy for the Battle of Chickamauga.

4. You can roll pension funds into slush funds without running up a big cleaning bill.

5. The Federal Deposit Insurance Corporation will reimburse you up to $100,000 if, during a run on the banks, your savings passbook is shredded by a crazed shopping bag lady.

After sifting through the responses, Marylebone classified them into three distinct personality traits, which he termed Type A, Type B, and Go Away We're Closed. Type A personalities, when told, for instance, that ten minutes ago Russia launched two hundred intercontinental ballistic missiles aimed at the United States, are likely to cover their faces with their hands and blubber, "Oh God, Oh God, Oh God." Type B's, on the other hand, will invariably ask themselves, How can I use this information to get out of paying this month's Master Charge bill?

Once you have determined what type you are, you will know what course to take. If you are Type A, this book really doesn't concern you, and you may as well stop reading here. And if you think you're entitled to a refund, Mack, just try and get one.

For Type B's, however, the prospects are bright—*if* you are willing to use your God-given wits, take some risks, and forget everything you ever learned about the Judeo-Christian ethic.

How the World Will End

If we could penetrate the mists of prehistory, we would see that humans have always been preoccupied with apocalyptic presentiments. Or, to put that in plain English, people have always been worried about the end of the world. From primitive man (and woman), spooked by eclipses of the sun, to medieval man (and woman), cowering before the Black Death, to modern man (and woman), facing the prospect of nuclear annihilation, great significance has always been placed on the interpretation of omens (and owomens). More surprising is that, from the very outset, some people have tried to capitalize on doomsday anxiety and succeeded.

Testimony to this contention may be seen in the form of a crudely inscribed piece of water buffalo scat discovered by a team of anthropologists headed by Annamarie Yerb of the Parsons School of Design. This wonderful find, called the Serengeti Puckey, may be seen in the Scatology Wing of New York City's Museum of Natural History. It describes the concern evinced by a middle-aged *Australopithecus erectus* that impinging glaciation was creating a bearish decline in hartebeests, whose liver, kidneys, and other kishkes were prized by these humanoids. The Serengeti Puckey goes on to tell how a member of the tribe whose name loosely translates to Stanislaus Wysocki had been speculating on these innards to the annoyance of the rest of the tribe, which had thereupon beaten his brains to bouillabaisse with heavy rocks.

So there is nothing new about doomsday worries. It's just that the world is more complex. But try and get a good piece of hartebeest liver for under $3.79 a pound.

As we bend our vision to the future, we may perhaps feel twinges of dread not dissimilar to those experienced by our primitive ancestors at the prospect that the Big Short-Order Chef in the Sky is going to eighty-six life on this planet as we have known it. Perhaps we should pause here to examine the ways in which the world will end.

Those of us with classical educations are familiar with the commonly depicted "Four Horsemen" of the Apocalypse, namely, Famine, War, Pestilence, and Sneezy. We know they're saddled up and stomping anxiously around the starting gate. How will they manifest themselves—and when?

There are four major schools of thought, which because of their proximity have formed the Apocalypse League, with spirited competition in badminton, lacrosse, and Johnny-Jump-the-Pony. Now, what are the philosophies of these schools?

Well, some say the world will end in fire, some say ice. Some say the world will end in a bang, some say a whimper.

Fire. Advocates of the fire school maintain that extraterrestrial influences will cause tens of millions of people to fall asleep while smoking in bed.

Ice. Ice advocates say that (thanks to the same extraterrestrial influences) a massive polar ice cap will descend on the planet, covering all land areas with deep ice and canceling skiing for the season.

Bang. The Bang school is divided into two subgroups, the Big Bangers and the Little Bangers. We know about the Big Bang theory of the end of the world, but the Little Bang is considerably more abstruse. However, since the Little Bang is supposed to go off about fifteen minutes before the Big Bang, the distinction seems immaterial.

Whimper. Finally, there are the Whimperians, who believe that one day, everyone in the world will just sit down wherever they may be and say, "Aw, screw it."

There are lesser schools of thought on the subject, such as the one predicting a deadly meteor shower, or the one predicting a fatal breakdown of the ecosystem, or the one predicting the destruction of the ozone layer over the planet, or the one predicting nuclear power plant disasters. An astronomer has prognosticated an earth-moon collision in four billion years (don't look so distressed: he said four *billion,* not four *million),* and a biologist says he is certain there will be a killer virus in our time.

A theory currently making the rounds posits that the world will simply stop spinning and everything will fly off and fall into the sun, except for Los Angeles which will become a satellite of Mars. There is ample evidence even now that the world is slowing down. Researchers at the Furtwangler Institute for Advanced Studies and Horseshoe Instruction observed that the average waiting time for a boccie court in Dubuque has lengthened from ten minutes in 1960 to six hours in 1980. Yet the incidence of sunstroke has increased exponentially, except in women's doubles. These startling data have been rationalized into the following formula:

$$\frac{C^2 - B(31 \times G^4)}{M + f - 6 \times v}$$

8

* * *

In this formula, C equals the number of times the earth turns on its axis daily, B is the number of times it spins on weekends and holidays, G is the height of the Jungfrau, M is for the many things you gave me, f—6 is the proper camera stop for a group photo of the Dubuque boccie team (Won 7–Lost 2), and v is a typographical error—it should have been w.

There is another theory that after an extremely wet winter followed by an extremely arid summer, so much pollen will be released into the air that the entire human race will be convulsed in a giant allergy attack and will thus perish. Still another theory predicts world war on a scale never before witnessed. I am quite familiar with world geopolitics, having taken the Fugazy World Geopolitics Package Tour ("Fourteen Violence-and Terrorism-Filled Days, Fifteen Social Unrest and Leftist-Leaning Nights"), and I can safely predict that if world war does break out, it will commence with the assassination of an archduke in some obscure Balkan country.

Many lesser theories abound about how the world will end. This particular brand of paranoia has been institutionalized in the literature of Survivalists, a growing cult of well-provisioned and well-armed individuals dedicated to the proposition that Civilization Will Definitely Fail in Our Time. At any given assemblage of Survivalists, you may hear advocates of viral pandemics, international power blackouts, worldwide strikes, mass hysteria, mass suicide, and mass transit. One Survivalist believes the most important tool you can salvage from the Final Collapse is a lathe, for not only can you rebuild homes and factories with it, you can make other lathes with it as well. Unfortunately, he has become gravely worried that a master race of lathes will then take over the world.

At any rate, the important thing . . . excuse me, but this statement is worthy of its own heading:

The Important Thing

The important thing is not knowing how the world will end, but when. Let me repeat that.

The Important Thing

The important thing is not knowing how the world will end, but when.

So? When is it Going to End?

Just hold your horses. I'll get to it when I'm good and ready.

But You Just Said . . .

I know what I just said. Look, Jack, one more word out of you and I'll have you ejected from this book.

I'm Sorry

That's better.

Now, I happen to know exactly when the world will end, but I wouldn't want to spoil the surprise, and besides, it would kill sales of my newsletter if I told. I can, however, tell you what to look for. Some signs are rather obvious: you'll hear a lot of trumpets, you'll see the earth giving up its dead, lions lying down with lambs, men beating swords into plowshares, rain falling for forty days and forty nights, angels flying all over the place, and masses of people running hysterically against traffic on Madison Avenue, rending their garments. There'll be an assortment of distresses like pestilence, boils, locusts, and murrain (whatever that is), plus some rather unsettling weather disturbances like hail, whirlwinds, and a variation on drought called drouth.

The trouble with all this is that by the time it happens, it'll be much too late to do you any good. Once you see the earth giving up its dead, for instance, figure you have half an hour before it's all over, Charlie.

But there are lesser-known—and, indeed, arcane—signs of the coming end which you, in the privacy of your own home, can interpret to your everlasting enrichment. Well, not everlasting, exactly, but certainly longer than half an hour. So commit the following inside information to memory. Later in the book, we'll show you how you can use it to steal a march on your fellowman.

The best way to tell that the end is imminent is to observe the animals. It is commonly known that certain creatures are supersensitive to fluctuations in the electromagnetic fields in their environment, even though those fluctuations are undetectable to humans. When those fields are disturbed, however subtly, these creatures will react with uncustomary behavior.

It has been documented, for example, that seacows are able to sense forthcoming tidal waves days before the event is detected by humans. Indeed, for humans the first detectable sign of a tidal wave is the arrival of a forty-five-foot fishing ketch on their sun porch. But seacows anticipate these giant waves by abruptly going off their feed. From a normal diet of watercress and seaweed, seacows will change to center-cut pork chops, onion rings, broccoli with cheese sauce, and endive salad with house dressing.

What has this to do with the end of the world? Simple: there are numerous end-of-the-world animal behavior syndromes which are observable by any jerk with just a few hours of practice daily in the home!

The more prominent of these are:

1. Hereford cattle begin talking Yiddish. Not a lot, mind you—just what is known as a *shmoos,* or as a cow might put it, *schmoooos.*

2. Lemmings congregate in San Francisco's Ghirardelli Square and march on Gump's department store.

3. Certain breeds of dog, notably Pomeranians, develop an inexplicable but intense loathing for spinach-and-bacon quiche.

4. One week before the prime rate jumps by 10 percent, Rhode Island Red hens stop laying jumbo eggs and start laying jumbo jets.

What Exactly Am I Supposed to Do With This Information?

First, get yourself a Hereford cow. Sure, it's inconvenient, but not as inconvenient as losing all your hard-earned money in some apocalypse, right?

Most likely you live in the city, where cattle are hard to find, let alone maintain. In my newsletter you'll find a list of places in major urban areas where you can buy Hereford cows and starter sets of hay, bridles, milk pails, hoof-and-mouth disease, and the like.

One way to ease the cost of a cow is for tenants in an apartment building to buy and own one cow cooperatively. That way, one person would always be in Bossy's stall at any given time, monitoring her for incipient outbreaks of Yiddish. Or, if your building has no cattle stalls, convert the bicycle room or tether her to the boiler. Now you're all set. As soon as that cow says, *"Oy vay, 's'iz Yom Hadin"* ("Uh-oh, it's the end of the world"), you'll know it's time to put your investment strategy into effect.

HOW TO KNOW IF THE END OF THE WORLD IS NIGH
Hereford cows start speaking Yiddish.

If a cow is absolutely out of the question because your kid is allergic or something, then a viable alternative is to contact someone in San Francisco and ask him to keep an eye out for lemmings gathering in Ghirardelli Square. As soon as it happens, pow!—you act!

Of course, you may not know anybody in San Francisco, or even if you do, this person might not know what a lemming looks like. Lemmings do look remarkably like voles, and you wouldn't want to launch your investment strategy prematurely because some dingaling couldn't tell a vole from a lemming.

For city dwellers, then, perhaps the easiest thing is to buy a chicken and wait for it to start pecking amorously at a Boeing 747. Or if that's no good, buy that Pomeranian. Feed it an exclusive diet of spinach-and-bacon quiche and watch it from behind your refrigerator. The very instant it turns its nose up at quiche, run, don't walk, to your investment broker and say the code word that you and he cooked up for just such a contingency. That code word, by the way, should be kept as simple and memorable as possible, like "rufous" or "futtock." Keep away from complicated espionage phrases like, "An east wind blows off the Urals," with their equally complicated recognition phrases like, "Yes, but you should see what's doing in the Carpathians!"

For further information, drop a line to the Acme Livestock Leasing Company in Ghirardelli Square, San Francisco. Ask for my brother-in-law Morty.

'Tis a Pity She's a Hoarder

"Maybe on my income I could buy half a Kruger-rand, but three years ago I bought $360 worth of tuna fish. It cost 37 cents a can. We're using it up, and I have to replace it at 75 cents now, so you can see it works out."

—NANCY LITWACK, proprietress,
survival supply store

How often have you heard your friends complain that they can't get a good piece of _____ any more. If you'll fill in the blank with a few of your favorite things, you'll see that you really *can't* get a good piece of it any more. We're running out of everything, except people who complain they can't get anything any more. Where have all the good pieces gone?

Well, so many of life's desirables have been depleted by demand that supplies are nearly exhausted. A good piece of swordfish, a good piece of veal, a good piece of ivory, a good fox fur coat—all, all no longer available except at a premium. Take titanium or beryllium—have you tried to buy some lately? Have you looked at the prices they're getting? What do you mean, you don't need any titanium or beryllium?

Or take rhinocerous horn. Because it's prized in the fabled East (particularly Baltimore) as an aphrodisiac, it is no longer available anywhere in the world except the appetizer counter in Bloomingdale's gourmet department. It is said that just a tad of rhinoceros horn in your lover's tea, coffee, or vanilla malted will make that person bonkers with desire. Based on personal observation, I must dispute this contention. First of all, the goddamn thing must weigh fifty pounds! Have you ever hoisted a fifty-pound rhino horn up to a table and dipped it suavely into a Spode teacup? Can't be done.

Second of all, it's disgusting to look at, all covered with rough matted hair. Yuck! If rhinoceros horn puts your lover in the mood for romance, don't bother fixing me up with any of your friends. If I want to get someone aroused, I'll stick to my traditional aphrodisiac, camphor balls. You drop a camphor ball into a girl's teacup, she's your slave for life. And you can usually find them at Bloomingdale's appetizer counter, too.

Other commodities are still available in abundance, but because they are prohibitively expensive, they might as well be unavailable, for all the good they do us. These fall into the Don't Touch That Or I'll Call the Police category, and they follow the classic formula laid down by John Smith, brother of the more prominent economic theorist Adam Smith. Because of his common name, John's work was always being passed over by scholars, who often asked him rude questions like, "Weren't you married to Pocahontas once?" or "Wasn't that your name I saw on the register of the No-Tell Motel the other day? How's *Mrs.* Smith, heh, heh?" John did, however, come up with one brilliant theory about the dynamics of economies that has become an axiom throughout the civilized world.

Smith's formula is elegantly simple: when demand goes up and supply goes down, grand theft auto rises precipitously. Of course, in Smith's day they had no autos—the phrase was "grand theft coach and four"—but I've adapted the original to modern usage. Smith took his theory quite far, refining it to the point where he could state with confidence, "For every thirty pounds of cockles sold in the East End, some dutchess is going to find her carriage nicked." Astonishingly, he was proven right time after time and was awarded the Order of the Purple Cockle. Alas, he collected it posthumously, for he died one Sunday afternoon of hepatitis after dining on tainted mussels in the Fox and Hatband. The inn was closed for health violations a week later (cited for mouse excreta in the Yorkshire Pudding).

Smith's theory is still valid today. The relationship between the price of bay scallops (the closest thing we have to cockles) and reports of stolen Lincoln Continental Mark V's (the closest thing we have to coaches and four) is constant within two ounces of scallops or one hubcap of car.

What this means is that as we approach the exhaustion point of our resources, prices will take off into the blue. A typical grocery list of tomorrow will look something like this Plutzling-Rundinker projection:

ScotTissue .... $5,500 roll

Fleischmann's Margarine............ $17,500 1-lb package

Minute Maid Orange Juice............... $6,300 6-oz can

Wesson Oil .... $40,000 gallon

Head & Shoulders .... $9,000 bottle

Breast & Buttocks .... $12,500 bottle

Janitor in a Drum .... $15,000 gallon

Cleaning Lady in an 9 oz can............ $10,000 9-oz can

Valet in a Jar, Thursday evenings and Sundays off .. $3,111
gallon

Handi Wrap................................ $2,500 roll

Inconvenient Wrap......................... $1,500 roll

Borden Singles .... $95,000 1-lb package

Borden Couples .... $75,000 1-lb package

Borden Young Marrieds .... $15,000 1-lb package

Borden Married, Filing Separately ... $10,000 1-lb package

Red Delicious Apples. .... $4,500 lb

Gray Insipid Apples .... $1,500 lb

Brown, Shriveled, Rotten Apples .... $950 lb

The above prices may vary by eight or nine hundred dollars depending on location, but, generally speaking, we can look forward to the fifty-thousand-dollar oil change, the thirty-thousand-dollar training bra, and the one-hundred-thousand-dollar Tupperware set.

A bagel, cream cheese, and lox will cost $400,000, and that's not even Nova Scotia—that's belly! You even have to pay $20,000 extra for a piece of sliced onion. If deli waiters are rude at today's prices, can you imagine their insolence when you ask for a slice of onion a couple of years from now? And they'll still have the nerve to expect a $30,000 tip!

Rapidly rising prices create a situation accurately predicted in Smith's Law, Part Two (starring Jane Fonda, Warren Beatty, and Sissy Spacek, with Ann-Margret as the President's mistress). This law states that when the wage-price index reaches parity with the price-earnings ratio of twenty-five selected Dow-Jones industrials (adjusted to account for injured brokers), people will begin hoarding.

The process of hoarding is an ancient one. The first recorded instance is the famous Cuneiform in the Uniform, a series of economic essays printed on the hem of a ceremonial outfit worn by a Chaldean princess buried in the Ziggurat of Ur-Um located at the confluence of these two rivers, you know which ones I mean, the real famous ones? The princess had been put to death in a particularly cruel fashion (her nostrils stuffed with walnut meats), but a common one prescribed for "bnubnu," or hoarding. At least, we suppose that's what "bnubnu" means, but it might also be interpreted as batting left-handed. The princess, it seems, had been hoarding, but precisely what she'd been hoarding is a matter of conjecture. A clue is provided in the cuneiform "Yeggi," which means limelight. So that's it: the princess had been "hoarding" (hogging) the limelight at a time when limelight in Ur-Um was in critical demand, and if you don't agree with this interpretation, *you* go spend twenty-five years translating "Yeggi bnubnu groog O plobba drdfnd"! Jesus, give an archaeologist a break!

Many people I know say they feel guilty about hoarding. They feel it's un-American to stockpile food and fuel when their neighbors are going without. I tell them, "Don't call it hoarding. Think of it as saving for a rainy day." They feel much better after that. I recently bumped into a friend in front of a Key Food supermarket, and she was loading boxes into a fourteen-wheel ten-ton cross-country moving van. "What have you got there?" I asked.

"Six hundred one-pound packages of Soft Parkay Margarine,

fourteen hundred twelve-ounce packages of Ritz Crackers, one hundred six-packs of Schaefer beer, three hundred fifteen-ounce jars of Mott's Applesauce, seven hundred eleven-ounce packages of Sunshine Vanilla Wafers, one thousand ten-ounce jars of Maxwell House Instant Coffee, and fifteen hundred thirteen-ounce cans of Bumble Bee Tuna," she replied with a wry smile.

"Hoarding?" I asked.

"Sit-down dinner for ten," she replied with a wink. She didn't feel strange about it because she didn't call it hoarding, so remember that it's not what you do, it's what you call it that counts. We'll be applying this lesson later in the book in our discussions of rape, murder, and looting.

Hoarding is not much of a problem in the country, where there is lots of room to stockpile your acquisitions. But it can present severe headaches to city dwellers who scarcely have enough room for a coffee table, let alone one thousand jars of coffee. A number of urbanites have solved this problem creatively by integrating stock-piled materiél into their decor.

For instance, six crates of Kretchmer Wheat Germ (twelve-ounce

SUCCESSFUL STOCKPILING
Replace sofa cushions with 20-lb. bags of Extra Long Grain Rice and
brightly colored slipcovers.

jars) covered with a tablecloth can easily pass for a dining table. Your legs may be a little cramped at dinner time, and your plates may tend to slide into your lap when you begin taking jars out of the crates. Nevertheless, it's a cunning way to camouflage thirty or forty pounds of wheat germ, you have to admit.

By the same token, you can replace sofa cushions with twenty-pound bags of Extra Long Grain Carolina Rice—with bright slipcovers, no one will know the difference. Just watch out for humid days, because your sofa may swell to three or four times its normal size.

A little cleverness can go a long way. Two half-pound Hebrew National salamis make wonderful bookends, and a pyramid of twelve-ounce cans of Green Giant Corn Niblets can easily replace that ugly vase of artificial flowers. Take it as far as imagination can stretch. Friends may guffaw when you replace your bedroom pillows with coffee- or tea-filled trash-can liners, or your queen-sized mattress with two hundred five-pound bags of Pillsbury flour, but when the bad times hit and these selfsame friends come around begging for a piece of your freshly baked bread, you can slam the door in their faces and gloat, "Go spread some butter on your Sealy Posturepedic!"

And speaking of mattresses, one author recommends water beds for the entire family on the grounds that in a crisis you have an instant source of cooking and drinking water—*if* you filter out the copper sulfate that is added to water-bed water to inhibit the growth of algae. In our family, however, we keep the copper sulfate in our water supply, for, combined with the sodium nitrate, disodium guanylate, monosodium glutamate, and thiamin hydrochloride in our emergency rations, it not only keeps our bodies algae-free, but has an effect very much akin to ganja cut with ethyl alcohol.

You may find yourself with more of certain "rainy day" products than you really need and may want to dispose of them. Obviously, in these days of quadruple-digit inflation, you'll be able to sell them for a profit. And that's just what you're going to do.

The process has been called black market profiteering by critics. But who are they, anyway? Just a bunch of have-nots too dumb to have stockpiled goods when they had a chance. Well, as my grandfather used to say, "Scratch a critic and you'll find a bootlegger." You're not going to become a black marketeer, you're simply going to be engaging in a little redistribution of surpluses at current market prices. If you bought a jar of Smucker's Strawberry Preserves a year ago at $1.39 and resell it today for fifteen hundred dollars, does that make you a bad person? No! You're just going with the irresistible flow of supply and demand. Nevertheless, it's a good idea to pack a sturdy sidearm when conducting your negotiations, as everyone may not appreciate the flow of supply and demand as keenly as you do.

Your job in the coming months, then, will be to study the market and decide which consumer goods and commodities are going to be in great demand in the coming hard times. Start accumulating them now, but try to think things through before you begin your acquisition program. For instance, you may have difficulty selling off your surplus banana yogurt four years after its on-sale date. But who knows? To paraphrase P. T. Barnum, there's a buyer of four-year-old banana yogurt born every minute.

A Man's Home Is His Bunker

"You got to figure $1,000 for a month's food for a family. Another $300 to $500 for radios . . . Weapons? The sky's the limit."
    —MIKE MCKINNEY, survival consultant

A dozen times a day I'm asked: in these uncertain times, is it better to live in the city or the country? I always answer with Montaigne's witty parable of the bull moose and the prairie chicken, which plainly illustrates the drawbacks of both country and city living. I've lived in both during bad times and can tell you, for instance, that if you're bankrupt and want to hurl yourself out of a window, an apartment building fifteen stories high lends itself to that purpose far better than a farmhouse. On the other hand, if you're ducking out of your back window to escape creditors, the first floor of a colonial is where you want to be.

In the city, you're more likely to be victimized by forces beyond your control, such as one-day closeout sales in Lord & Taylor's handbag department. In the country, such things rarely happen, but then in the country you can't send out for Chinese. If you live in a country home, you can burn it down for the insurance with impunity. If you burn down your apartment building, however, you have all those nagging worries about manslaughter.

I have weighed the pros and cons. A good pro weighs about one hundred eighty pounds on the average, whereas cons tend to go over two hundred. But after weighing both, I've concluded that, *au fond,* a small town is the place to live in hard times. In fact, I've settled in Au Fond, Nebraska, "Home of the Corn-Fed Tortoise." It's a lovely town with rolling, golden meadows splashed with shade from tall elms, an old-fashioned main street with friendly bucolic types waving cheerfully from every doorway, a decent place where ethnic minor-

IN THESE UNCERTAIN TIMES, IS CITY OR COUNTRY
THE BEST PLACE TO LIVE?
Apartment balconies are recommended for suicides faced with bankruptcy.
But if you have to duck out the back window to escape creditors, the
ground floor of a colonial is where you want to be.

ities are either excluded, barely tolerated, or harassed beyond endurance. If you're ever passing through, y'all just drop by and see us, hear? Just walk through the metal detector with your hands up where I can see them.

One thing I like about rural areas is that country property is an excellent inflation hedge, whereas in most city apartments there isn't enough light to grow an inflation hedge or any other kind of hedge. I couldn't even get a goddamn marginata to grow in mine!

For another thing, you can be more self-sufficient in the country. If you run out of food, you just go into the barn and slaughter one of your pigs. You run out of food in the city, what can you slaughter? Only Bobby's hamster and one or two black mollies, if they haven't already died of ick.

A third thing has to do with disposal of you-know-what in an emergency. City dwellers are fairly sophisticated about the recycling of bottles, aluminum cans, and other household waste products. But when it comes to you-know-what, once they've fertilized the African violets in their kitchen window, urbanites have pretty much exhausted their ingenuity. There is no you-know-what problem in the country.

A fourth reason is, there are more places to hide in the country—silos, woodsheds, outhouses, curing houses, ice houses, barns, chicken coops, and so on. Now, where can you hide in an apartment? Your coat closet? You can't even get *coats* into your coat closet, for crying out loud, let alone your wife and kids and rations for six months. And when those bands of lust-maddened rioters burst into your apartment, don't you think they're going to look in your coat closet first?

Finally, a country property makes a much better fortress than an apartment. Most leases will not permit tenants to bring 75-millimeter howitzers into an apartment, and even if yours does, many movers won't carry anything heavier than a .50 caliber machine gun upstairs unless you pay them an exorbitant shmear. Union regulations.

Now that you've decided to move to the country, how do you implement your decision?

The first thing you must do is sell your city apartment. Yes, you'll object, but I don't *own* my city apartment, I just rent. That's the sort of fuzzy thinking that put you behind the eight ball in the first place.

Of *course*, you don't own your apartment, dummy, but do you really have to tell that to a buyer? If a prospective purchaser says to you, "May I please examine the title to your property?" your reply should be, "What do I look like, some kind of thief?" He'll be so intimidated, you'll soon have him begging to sign any paper you put before him. By the time he wises up, you'll be living like a sheik in your new country home. A list of states with weak extradition laws may be found in the October 1978 issue of my newsletter.

If you do own your apartment, you're really in clover. Here's what you do: when a prospect makes you an offer, take his down payment and tell him the closing is in a week. The next day, do the same thing with another buyer. In a few weeks you'll have sold your apartment ten or fifteen times. Anyone wants to see your deed, you can show it to him—nothing to hide. If you can get cash, you don't even have to report it to the Internal Revenue Service, and all you have to worry about is being waylaid while carrying four or five hundred thousand dollars in small bills. As soon as possible, you should convert that cash into another liquid commodity, like champagne.

While you're taking care of business in the city, your mate should be out in the country surveying properties for your ideal rural home. Your criteria will be extremely strict. The property must be far from any designated first-strike target in the Kremlin's grim scenario for world domination, but close enough to the city for you to take in a Yankee game. The population should be 82,004, which demographers agree is the optimum number because it is divisible by 19. (Don't bother—the answer is 4,316.)

The town should not be overly dependent on one crop, such as filbert nuts, because if there is a major disruption in the food distribution system in the nation, you're going to get goddamn good and tired of filbert nuts. The town should be located near plentiful supplies of wood, water, and toilet paper. It should stand on an unassailable bluff and be surrounded by unfordable rivers. All approaches should be protected by cannon loaded with grapeshot. If possible, the town should be entirely walled and patrolled by sentries armed with pikes and crossbows.

I know of only one town that meets all of these criteria, and that's Au Fond, Nebraska, where myself, the missus and our kids, our incredibly vicious Doberman Thor, our dusky indentured servants Rastus and Becky, and Rachel, our Yiddish-speaking Hereford cow, live. I do know of some terrific properties still available, so if you're interested, you should contact Coming Hard Times Rural Homes, Inc. Just ask for my niece Wanda.

Negotiating For Your Country Home

Once you've found your ideal country home, you'll often discover that the asking price isn't as firm as the seller would like you to think it is. You might try the following ploy that worked well for me.

Offer the seller one-twentieth of what he's asking for his home. When he turns you down with a chortle, start a rumor that the state is building a low-security correctional facility for sex maniacs on the adjoining property. You'll undoubtedly be able to close your deal the following morning. And by the way, if you really want to squeeze every drop of profit out of your new home, you can claim high depreciation by *building* a low-security correctional facility for sex maniacs on the adjoining property!

Financing Your Country Home

How do you pay for your country home? Well, if you're as dumb as you look, you'll take all the cash you made on your city property and buy the country one with it. A better idea is to put a very small down payment on it—say, $3.50. You then take out a big mortgage, using your daughter as collateral. Now you have a lot of cash, and all you need are some investment opportunities and a good bail bondsman. We'll be describing those investment opportunities later in the book, but tell me, how are you enjoying it so far? Terrific, huh? Let's have a big hand for this book!

I'm often asked whether fixed-rate mortgages are better than those with variable rates. It depends on who's fixing the rates. In most banks and savings-and-loan institutions, the same people who fix mortgage rates are the ones who fix college basketball games. Variable rates aren't much more dependable, however, as they're pegged to such things as the last three digits of the winning number in the New Jersey lottery.

Decorating Your Country Home—
Some Do's and Don'ts

As soon as the deed is signed, set up your gun emplacements and lay down your barbed wire and mine fields. Here are some helpful hints that my family and I have picked up in the course of our experiences.

Do make sure the tires are inflated on your mobile antitank guns. There is nothing so embarrassing as that flop-flop-flop sound of a deflated tire as you quickly try to reposition your gun in a siege.

Do set up your machine guns at right angles to each other. That way, in case your defense perimeters are breached and you are assailed by waves of predatory urban refugees, you can cut them down with a hail of vicious crossfire. Don't do as my late Uncle Abner and Aunt Winnie did, which was to set up their machine guns *opposite* each other. Abner and Winnie never did know much about country living.

Do leave a spare copy of your mine field map to a trusted member of your family, so that if God forbid something should happen to you, your family can make its way out or your visitors can make their way in without unpleasant incidents. Nothing can spoil a cocktail party faster than the inadvertent setting off of a mine by a guest.

Do keep a potty chair in your armored personnel carrier if you have very young infants. When you're rushing to rescue besieged friends and little Danny has to tinkle, you'll bless me for making you remember.

Don't throw away your old beer bottles. Break them and mix them with mortar, then spread the mixture along the top of the retaining wall around your property. Anyone tries to intrude on your privacy, presto!—deep gashes and lacerations!

Don't run your toaster while your electric fence is on, as it tends to weaken the electric jolt delivered to your attacking neighbors.

Don't try to pull the pins of hand grenades out with your teeth. That's strictly Hollywood stuff. And don't forget to count to six before throwing. Better make that three—you look like a nervous type.

SECURITY FOR YOUR RURAL FORTRESS
Claymore mines discourage desperate refugees, but cocktail guests should
be issued minefield maps.

Don't try to handle a flamethrower unless you really know what you're doing. We once set my Cousin Wilma on fire, and it was hell putting her out.

And finally, for God's sake, test which way the wind is blowing before setting off your teargas canisters. There's always one hothead who forgets in the heat of battle, and dumb stunts like that can really play hob with your defense of high ground.

An Emergency Larder

In the cellar of your home you should build a larder and stock it heavily with emergency rations. It should be made out of reinforced concrete and booby-trapped in case Grandpa gets hungry in the middle of the night—nothing that'll really harm him, mind you, just something to remind him that the larder is for emergencies only.

What should you stock your larder with? Well, you can start with lard, I suppose, but our subterranean pantry contains such staples as potato flakes, dried beans, dehydrated foods and coffee, salted and tinned meat, canned soups, canned vegetables and canned fruits, rice, crackers, bottled water and juices, canned tuna, bags of sugar, boxes of salt, sacks of flour, and crates of beer and wine. I have also secreted a cache of black jelly beans, for when things get rough I have a rage for black jelly beans. What other staples do you need? I suggest Swingline, as dried beans tend to jam staple machines and don't do a very good job of holding two pieces of paper together.

Food supplements like vitamins and protein powder are desirable, but if none is available, try supplementing your diet with a long swig of Johnny Walker Red Label.

We also store lots of edible weeds and roots in our cellar. Bear in mind that unpalatable does not mean inedible. If your chestnut tree roots taste like a recently patched inner tube, you obviously are not adding enough carob syrup. We keep lots of medicine for common ailments like flu and strep throat, and more exotic remedies like opium salts to deaden the agonies of radiation burns in the event our home is near ground zero in a nuclear confrontation. Birth control pills, too; it could be a long stay.

It is important that you maintain a balanced diet while waiting out the coming crisis. Most nutritionists recognize four building blocks of sound diet. These are: proteins, carbohydrates, vitamins, and Ruffles. You must therefore build a balanced emergency larder in which each of these building blocks is adequately represented. An ideal meal might therefore look something like this:

Protein.............................Hot Dog

Carbohydrates.....................French Fries

Vitamins ....Pickle Relish

Ruffles ....Ruffles

A family can survive for a long time on such a nutritionally balanced diet. Mine, for instance, survived on it through a Baltimore-Cleveland doubleheader in which both games ran into extra innings, plus there was a two-hour rain delay in the fourth inning of the second game, when men were stranded on first and second base with two outs and the go-ahead run at the plate. Obviously, though, some variety must be provided in one's diet, particularly if your home is going to be under siege for any appreciable length of time, or if you have to wait for several months until postwar radiation subsides to an acceptable level. Every once in a while, then, you might substitute a hamburger, beans, sweet relish, and Ruffles.

Food storage is complicated by the problem of shelf life. In a recent study at the University of Kamchatka Agriculture Department and Women's Gym, experimenters determined the four stages in the deterioration of a plate of franks and french fries left on the shelf of their laboratory near the preserved coyote pancreases:

1. After one hour, the franks turn gray, the fries go limp.

2. After twenty-four hours, relish begins to congeal. Flies begin investigating.

3. After thirty-six hours, flies take things very seriously. Lab technicians begin to sniff the air and ask, "What died? Did something die?"

4. After seventy-two hours—don't ask.

One question that comes up frequently in connection with shelf life of foods is, What if I don't have any shelves? The easiest way to deal with this problem is to use the simple formula:

$$SL = \frac{M^2 \times fm}{b \times d} + \frac{sp}{u}$$

In the above formula, SL stands either for Shelf Life, Soft Lenses, or Sidney Lumet; M^2 is Square Meal; fm is number of family members; b is the number of bacteria; d is the number of days since you bought the food; sp is the number of stomach pumps in use at any given time; and u stands for undertaker. The most important number is bacteria count, which you can easily ascertain by tapping the can with a soup spoon and counting the seconds until the can taps back. The faster the response, the faster you're going to chuck that can in the garbage or, if you're particularly shrewd, sell it to some unsuspecting beggar outside the walls of your country estate. The best way to keep bacteria count low, though, is to rotate your cans often. Be sure to rotate them on their axis and not on their side or they'll roll off your shelves and scratch your formica counter tops.

You must not only store enough food for at least a one-year crisis, but fuel as well—to cook with, power your emergency generator, operate your Land Rover and armored personnel carrier, and recharge the batteries on your daughter's Baby Alive. The ideal fuel is gasoline, but, as it is dangerous to store gasoline in your house, many experts advise you to use methane, also known as swamp gas. The January 1977 issue of our newsletter tells you how to create a small swamp in your home, complete with alligators, whooping cranes, and cottonmouth moccasins.

It was recently reported that the Department of Agriculture is encouraging midwestern farmers to grow sugar beets, which when fermented produce "a disease-resistant, high-powered source" of fuel. The reason why this country isn't already running on beet-derived "gasohol" is gasohol's inability to resist disease. With a little care, however, you can keep your fuel quite healthy so that in an emergency your car doesn't come down with Asiatic flu or strep carburetor. Every night before closing the garage door, drop a little castor oil or milk of magnesia down your gas tank. Take its

30

COPING WITH THE ENERGY CRISIS
Storing gasoline can be dangerous. But a small swamp in your home is a
safe and reliable source of methane gas.

temperature every morning, and at the first sign of abnormality, add two Bufferin and three teaspoons of STP. If fever persists, call your garage mechanic.

In the event you are caught short with inadequate supplies of conventional fuel, you can burn rolled-up newspapers and magazines, though I prefer books. Particularly desirable for incineration are the following, as they will have outlived their usefulness:

> *You Can Profit From a Monetary Crisis* by Harry Browne
> *How to Prosper During the Coming Bad Years* by Howard Ruff
> *The Coming Credit Collapse* by Alexander P. Paris
> *How You Can Profit From the Coming Price Controls* by Dr. Gary North
> *How You Can Become Financially Independent By Investing in Real Estate* by Albert J. Lowry
> *After the Crash* by Dr. Geoffrey Abert

Survival Books, an outfit located (not surprisingly) in West Los

Angeles, actually sells a survival handbook that is specifically designed for burning in an emergency. Published by the American Outdoor Safety League, it comes in a plastic zip-lock bag convertible into a drinking cup. The book itself is deer-hunter orange for easy recognition by search parties, who might also be attracted to the mirror you can make out of its Mylar centerfold. While waiting for your rescuers, you can remove the staples and make fishhooks out of them. And when the sun goes down, the wax-impregnated cover will help you start a fire. You should read the contents before burning, however, as it has some tips on survival in the great outdoors.

In our effort to be self-sufficient, we have stocked a juicer, a butter churn, a grain grinder, a Coleman stove, spare auto parts, fishing tackle, and, of course, all the guns and ammo money can buy.

Our underground stronghold is simply but tastefully designed with an eye mainly to function. Everything has a double use: our bookshelves break down into bricks for throwing and boards for burning. Our black curtains double as shrouds, our white tablecloths as bandages or surrender flags. We use jerricans of gasoline as end tables, ammo boxes as coffee tables. Sandbags serve as couch cushions and sand-filled fire buckets as ashtrays. For the walls we have crossed swords and hand-carved, personalized gun racks, as well as pictures of Jeremiah and other favorite prophets of doom. For relaxation we play war games or board games like Monopoly, from which the paper money will serve as excellent scrip in the coming crisis.

Our garage is also a model of preparation. Besides an amphibious personnel carrier and a Land Rover, we have a customized, armor-plated Chevy Nova with turret-mounted twin machine guns and rear grenade launcher.

We're ready.

If you're really perspicacious, you'll accumulate a surplus of food, fuel, ammunition, and other things for bartering. We have spoken about the black market as an outlet for your hoarded goods, but the black market depends on money as the medium of exchange, and in the coming terrible times, money will be worthless to cold, starving people. So we may have to go on a trading economy for a while. But how do you determine the value of one item in exchange for another?

Here are some guidelines for traders in the coming hard times:

1 carton of Marlboros is the equivalent of 2 Roach Motels

1 Smith & Wesson .38 police special = 3 Maidenform Cross-Your-Heart bras

4 jars of Vita Creamed Herring = 2 oz Colombian grass

1 cup All-Tempa Cheer = 2 shots Gilbey's Gin

1 barrel Prell Concentrate = 3 end cuts rib roast, hold the béarnaise sauce

2 Barbara Cartlands = 1 teaspoon vanilla, 1 egg yolk, pinch of nutmeg

1 6-oz jar bing cherries (pitted) = 2 bleacher tickets to a San Diego Padres night game

5 containers Dannon Dutch Apple yogurt = 1 Volkswagen muffler, slightly dented

4 Mickey Mantles = 2 Willie Mays

4 Roger Marises = 1 Willie Mays, 1 Ted Williams, 2 cards to be named later, and an undisclosed amount of cash

You may also want to barter services for commodities or other services. For example:

Put in three nights of sentry duty every week for your neighbor in exchange for an antitank weapon with "smart" rockets.

Exercise a friend's snarling, bloodthirsty guard dogs in exchange for a hundred yards of barbed wire.

Offer to erect someone's reinforced concrete pillbox for twenty gallons of fresh milk or fifty pounds of anchovy paste.

Just keep in mind that the Internal Revenue Service considers barter income.

Fut Floats, Crouton Spots, and Other Investment Strategies for the Eighties

"The most common criticism of the PPP theory is that it doesn't consider all the factors that affect a currency's price . . . Conversely, a BOP deficit is taken to indicate a weak currency."
—HARRY BROWNE, *New Profits from the Monetary Crisis*

No matter how the world ends, the event will be preceded by runaway inflation. What is inflation? Inflation may be defined as an uncontrolled spiral of wage and price increases accompanied by constant bitching. *This* is too high, *that's* too high, the *other thing* is too high . . . bitch, bitch, bitch.

The roots of inflation go deep into the fabric of American society, and before you tell me that's a mixed metaphor, let me hasten to point out that in Skokie, Illinois, where I come from, roots actually do go into fabric. You get into a wool sweater in the morning in Skokie, Illinois, as likely as not you'll find some roots in it.

Anyway, the American ethic seems to be that deficit financing is desirable. The government does it, businesses do it, everyone else does it, so why shouldn't we do it, too? Debt is as American as covert operations in Southeast Asia.

Why have Americans plunged so deeply into debt? Economists have cited many reasons: our perpetual balance-of-payments deficit, the easy-money fiscal policy of the Federal Reserve, unhealthy consumer credit practices fostered by banks and stores, Eurodollar manipulation by the so-called Gnomes of Zurich, unconscionable profiteering by oil sheiks, the Iranian crisis, greedy demands by labor unions, unsound farm subsidies, and unrealistic municipal planning. These factors have been abetted, one psychologist says, by

33

a shift from the Depression mentality that dominated the thinking of the generation that grew up in the 1930s to the Boom mentality of those who grew up in the prosperous 1950s.

None of these explanations touches the core of the problem. The real reason for American indebtedness is the invention of those little slots in wallets for credit cards. Until then, you either had to pay cash for your purchases or carry your credit cards around held together with a rubber band that was always breaking and snapping against your tushy. The invention of the credit-card holder changed all that, and the dawning of the Age of Aquarius can be dated from that time.

Inflation affects everyone, from the richest citizen to the very detritus of humanity, as evidenced by the recent Derelicts' March on the White House. Last May, hundreds of thousands of bums from around the country assembled on the mall in Washington for a march—well, more like a stagger, actually—on the presidential residence to protest the declining value of the quarter, which for so long had been the standard currency among paupers, pegged as it was to the cup of coffee. Now, with coffee prices zooming out of sight, they were pressing their demand for passage of HR-6087, popularly known as the Minimum Handout Bill, which would require the following scale:

Simple plea for help	50¢
Special appeal ("For my sick Aunt Minnie")	75¢
Particularly charming appeal ("Can you spare something for a postprandial cordial?")	$1.00
Car windshield washed (driver's side only)	50¢
Car windshield washed (driver's and passenger's)	75¢
With clean rag	$1.00
Each additional window	35¢
Menacing shakedown	$2.50

The marchers were dispersed with offers of cheap muscatel.

Inflation has been likened to a thief who steals silently into your home each night and takes a little bit of your money. I think that's putting it too mildly. Inflation is a thief who knees you in the groin, slams you to the sidewalk, smacks you in the mouth with a rubber truncheon, rips the wallet out of the inside pocket of your sports jacket, and breaks the thumb and pinky of your right hand while forcibly removing your ring and wristwatch. For good measure, he kicks you in the throat and nabs your keys, which he uses to break into your home where he brutally rapes your wife, sodomizes your sister, and flashes at your five-year-old daughter, carries off everything you own, burns your home to the ground, and, to add insult to injury, urinates on your freshly planted azaleas. *That's* inflation!

When they talk about runaway inflation, economists always point to Germany in the 1920s, citing it as a classic case. Why do they point to Germany? The reason is that inflation there got completely out of hand, rising by tens and even hundreds of percentage points daily until the government's printed money became worthless, the government collapsed, and conditions were set for the rise of dictatorship. Critics using Germany cite similarities to the economy of the United States in the 1980s.

That's bunk.

The really pertinent lesson is that of Tierra del Fuego in the 1930s.

Throughout the nineteenth century, and for the first three decades

THE BITTER LESSON OF TIERRA DEL FUEGO IN THE 1930's
Poor balance of trade resulted in a glut of its principal resource, rancid yak butter, and the collapse of the government. It could happen here!

of the twentieth, this tiny country, whose economy is based on rancid yak butter, had achieved a favorable balance of trade with its neighbor, the O'Shaunessy family (I told you, Tierra del Fuego is a tiny country). For three tubs of yak butter, the O'Shaunessy family would trade Tierra del Fuego six dead condors from the western slopes of the Andes, which the Tierra del Fuegans use to stuff throw pillows for their annual throw pillow festival. People came from far and wide to indulge in nostalgic stories about the golden age of throw pillows (June 12–July 16, 1781) while drinking the national beverage, rusty water, or participating in such games as throw-pillow throwing, throw-pillow fights, condor-plucking bees, Step on the Macacque's Foot, etc.

In the 1930s, however, a baby condor boom precipitated a shortage of dead condors. The shortage threw the balance of trade into utter disarray. Almost immediately, the country's principal bank, the Third Savings and Trust Company of Tierra del Fuego, collapsed, precisely as the First Savings and Trust and the Second Savings and Trust had done. It seems that these banks were built with domes, but the architects had designed them poorly—with the domes inverted. These filled with rainwater during the wet season, and after one or two storms they eventually collapsed. The 1930s tragedy killed four customers, two tellers, and a bank officer demonstrating an electric broom. More people would have been killed had it not been three o'clock in the morning.

The government reacted by trying to impose controls, but you know how peasants react to controls. So, naturally, even more rigid controls were imposed. Five herds of rancid yaks were slaughtered and left on mountainsides to rot, which, believe me, they did. At last the inevitable happened: the President fell from office (he tripped on his way to the men's room), and the people rose up against him. This set the stage for the rise of a plutocracy—that is, a government based on old Pluto cartoons—and the banks were closed for five years. If World War II hadn't stimulated the economy (rancid yak butter being essential to the production of K-rations), who the hell knows what would have happened!

What can we learn from this cautionary tale? Caution, for one thing: when you enter Tierra del Fuego, remember to come to a full stop and look both ways before driving on. The more important lesson, however, is that inflation can go berserk without warning anywhere at any time. It happened in Germany, it happened in France, it happened in Italy. It even happened in Mozambique, a nation notable for its stable economy—the exchange rate remained at thirteen stables to the dollar for three hundred years until 1978, when speculators started unloading Mozambique stables for the more profitable Taiwanese paddocks.

Hedges

If you are not to be wiped out by runaway inflation, you must find some way for your assets to run away *with* inflation. That's where hedges come in.

What is a hedge? As everyone knows, certain commodities rise in value step by step with inflationary increases. Many of these are quite familiar to the reader—precious metals like gold, silver, and platinum; precious stones like diamonds and rubies; real estate; collectibles like antique furniture, coins, stamps, autographs, first editions, lithographs, Oriental carpets, manuscripts, miniatures, porcelain figurines, and antique cars; and investments like oil stocks and Treasury bills. Others are less obvious but no less important: cheesecloth, cous-cous, Raisinettes, and Bufferin, to name a few. Still other hedges are privet, bramble, and Benson and Benson and. If you had bought a couple of privet hedges in 1960, when the dollar was 1.0 on the Kreskin-Todentanz index, they would be worth five times more today. Plus, your hedge would have grown by 300 percent, entitling you to a capital gain should you want to sell it back to Nick's Country Nursery.

In brief, your survival strategy must include the acquisition of hedges against inflation; otherwise, to paraphrase a spokesman for the President, you might as well climb into the whizzer and pull the chain. Let's examine some hedges in detail.

Precious Metals

Generally speaking, precious metals are sound buys in inflationary times, but there are notable exceptions. Gold and silver may be counted on to rise against the falling dollar, escalating interest rates, and dropping stock market averages. *But*—they always fall against price hikes in garlic croutons. The reasons for this go deep into the twisted psyches of precious metals dealers and traders, but, believe me, the correlation is unassailable. Many canny speculators post themselves in the fourth aisle of Izzy's Superette off Wall Street every morning and anxiously wait for Ramon, Izzy's clerk, to announce the garlic crouton "spot" for the day. If it's up even a penny, they race to their phones shouting, "Sell! Sell!"

A second problem with precious metals is storage. With the dramatic rise of gold and silver prices, there has been such a run on safe-deposit boxes that almost none is to be had anymore. The alternatives are pretty unsatisfactory. Some people carry their gold and silver bullion in their pants pockets, which causes unsightly bulges. Others stash it in jelly and pickle jars in their refrigerators, only to learn that it was thrown out with the spoiled cauliflower when the housekeeper defrosted the freezer. Still others carry their bullion in a satchel and skulk through the streets brandishing revolvers, shouting, "Stand back or I'll blow you away, dude!" So— storage of precious metals is indeed a problem. One firm, Investment Rarities, Inc., manufactures a plastic pipe that you can fill with coins and bury in your backyard. A *Wall Street Journal* article recently reported on the popularity of storing precious coins in cesspools, outhouses, and basement sumps, thus refuting the Latin proverb that money has no odor *(pecunia non olet)*.

But the big reason why these metals are, in the long run, poor investments is their sudden and inexplicable molecular decay that renders them without warning into baser elements. This is one of the best-kept secrets in the financial world, and it has been suggested that the phenomenon has to do with atomic testing, seismic activity in the Aleutians, or the closing of the Brooklyn Navy Yard. Whatever it is, one day you're carrying gold and the next day you're carrying lead. Silver bullion turns to Herb-Ox bouillon, and platinum to styrofoam. So I urge you to unload these commodities before you find yourself a pauper overnight. The Riches to Rags Precious Metals Trading Company will buy everything you can turn in—just ask for my Aunt Sadie. She'll give you one-tenth of the market price, but isn't that better than to be caught holding styrofoam?

Real Estate

Real estate isn't nearly as good a hedge as gold, silver, or platinum, but then it doesn't turn to lead overnight, either. The problem is that it isn't as liquid as those assets, except perhaps for the two thousand acres of Florida land someone sold me which turned out to be the bottom of Biscayne Bay.

Nor does real estate appreciate in value at the same pace as other inflationary factors. Using the Izzy's Superette criterion, we see that for every inch of inflation on Izzy's charts, real estate goes up half an inch, whereas gold and silver go up seven-eighths of an inch. Garlic croutons go *down* seven-eighths of an inch, as previously indicated.

Still, if you can hold onto real estate and manage to get out of it just before the end of the world begins, you can do okay. It starts, of course, with your picking a good plot. What's a good real estate plot? Here's a good real estate plot:

> Boy meets girl. Boy buys a plot of real estate in central Florida as an engagement present. Plot turns out to be

REAL ESTATE CAN BE PROFITABLE—IF YOU FIND A GOOD PLOT

located in Okefenokee swamp. Girl stabs boy in spleen with bread knife.

How do you know the value of your real estate holdings? Unlike metals or currencies, you can't follow the "action" in the financial section of your newspaper, can you? Can you? Are you awake or am I talking to myself?

Harry Browne, in his *New Profits From the Monetary Crisis,* says that "a long-established rule of thumb is that a property is worth one hundred times its monthly rental." He then goes on to say that this rule of thumb "obviously isn't very precise." That's just what's wrong with these pundits. They lay the blame everywhere except where it should be laid, namely, the length of their thumbs. How do they expect to predict anything accurately if they measure it with different-sized thumbs? The Bureau of Weights and Measures in Washington, D.C., has a Standard Thumb. It is 24.567 millimeters long. It was taken off a Bulgarian tourist struck by a trolley car in Chicago in 1915 and is exhibited, perfectly preserved, on the third floor of the bureau between Robert's Rules of Order and Parkinson's Law.

Now that we know what the multiple is, we can ascertain the value of your real estate with complete precision. Take your property's area, measure the depth of the topsoil, and add the number of buildings on the lot. Subtract the square footage of your aluminum siding, which is a definite minus. Then multiply 24.567 (Standard Thumb) and deduct one hundred dollars, which is the cost of a bribe to the super. Divide by the inflationary rate posted on page seven of the financial section of the Sunday *New York Times,* (no, dummy, that's the score of the Rangers-Sabres game), make a left at the flashing light, and turn your calculations upside down. What do you see? If it looks like a little gnome with a beard, you've done something wrong. Go back to the flashing light and multiply by the federal discount rate. Federal discounts can always be found in the basement of the Treasury Building near the racks of marked-down war bonds. Are you writing this down?

Here is where your arithmetic gets a little tricky. Many banks have a usury ceiling, which is the limit on how much interest they may charge on loans. If this figure is more than three times your orthodontist's bill and you still can't meet your property taxes, you'd better sell that property fast. If you have a tenant living on it, unload the tenant, too. Calculate the price of the tenant (age times income times hat size), and work him into the deal as a miscellaneous closing cost. Some states prohibit the eviction of tenants over sixty-five if they can produce their Medicare cards. Well, you know what you have to do. The end of the world is coming, and you can't hold up a real estate deal for some old person.

Investments

What is the proper investment posture for the 1980s? Some say it is to be splayed over a barrel with buttocks spread. If that sounds like you, you must take a closer look at your portfolio. If it is scuffed and frayed and the buckle is loose, you're ready for a new one. You can't possibly hope to prosper in the coming bad times with a tatty portfolio.

The important thing any investor should know is that as interest rates go up, bond yields go down. Do you understand why? I'll bet it's been explained to you a thousand times, and you still can't grasp it. You probably don't understand price-earnings ratios, either, but at least it's not necessary to understand them in order to invest in the stock market. Nevertheless, let me explain that the price-earning's ratio is the relationship between the price of a stock and what your stockbroker is earning. If he's making eighty big ones a year, you listen to that fellow.

Price earnings, shmice earnings, if you don't understand the concept, there are other guidelines that are completely comprehensible, even to blockheads like certain people reading this book. These guidelines include the Dow Jones average, the Standard & Poor 400 Index, and Nutsy Ed Poudopolis's Favorite Commodity Pick-'Ems, which you can buy anywhere good racing forms are sold. It's generally agreed that when these indices bottom at 800, 100, and 3 for 69¢ respectively, you're supposed to buy because they presage a bull market.

Don't believe it. The only thing that presages a bull market is *the* bull market. I'm talking about the market for bulls. In every recession this country has ever endured, recovery came within three months of an upswing in the price of bulls. Bull prices are related to hay crops, demand for beef and dairy products, and the outlook for larger herds. A good way to calculate the prospects for economic upswing is, for every hundred dollars a bull fetches at auction, there will be sixty-five lovelorn cows. Divide the price by stud fee per servicing and you should come up with an index, adjusted for flatulent calves, that runs circles around Dow Jones.

Commodities

In view of the fact that the world will soon be ending, we should use the word "futures" with caution. There is no "future" in anything. But some short-term futures, as they are commonly understood, might prove profitable if you know when to get in and when to get out. The trick is to ascertain which indicators are the critical ones. Some knowledgeable traders, for instance, base their assessments of the future health of the economy on the amount of uncured bacon in cold storage. I find that indicator unreliable, however, because they're finding new cures for things every day, and I can't believe that the same nation that put a man on the moon can't find a cure for bacon.

I prefer to use an amalgamated index that goes like this:

Wheat flour (Chicago Board of Trade)

Butter. AA (Kansas City Board of Trade)

Yeast (Commodity Exchange in New York)

Sugar (New York Coffee and Sugar Exchange)

Salt (Salt Lake City Exchange)

Eggs, large white (Chicago Large White Egg Exchange)

Corn oil (Southwest Polyunsaturated Exchange)

Pinch of pepper (Pinch of Pepper Room, St. Louis
Exchange)

From here it's so simple, any child can figure it out. Blend the
above commodities, and when they begin to rise, roll them over.
Cover them with a damp cloth (New York Cotton Exchange, Damp
Cloth Division), and they'll rise to even greater heights. Place them
on a board (Chicago Board or Kansas City Board, either will do just
fine), and go over them with a rolling pin (Oregon Lumber
Exchange and Dry Cleaners). Allow them to rise one more time,
then place them in a medium oven (Duluth Medium Oven Exchange), and let them appreciate for one hour. Remove and serve
with coca (New York Cocoa Exchange).

Yield: 12 percent, and that's tax-free!

Foreign Currencies

The average investor doesn't like to fool around with foreign
currencies because the exchange rate calculations are too sophisticated. If someone comes up to you and says, "Pardon me, fella, but
do you have two Peruvian sols for a Kuwaiti dinar?" and your gut
reaction is to smash him on the cheekbone with a tire iron, you
probably ought not to be fooling around with foreign currencies.

Yet there are staggering fortunes to be made investing in other
nations' moneys. The secret is to be able to convert disparate
currencies without thinking twice. Had you, for instance, been able
to buy Saudi riyals with Danish krones, sell krones for Mexican
pesos, and trade your pesos for Ecuadorian sucres during the Illinois
Republican primary in March 1980, you'd have made a 2,000
percent profit. Instead, you sat around drinking beer, muttering, "I
don't know, I like Reagan, who do you like?"

If you'll take the trouble to study conversion tables and carry
around a Canon P10-D calculating machine, a pair of troy scales, ten
thousand dollars worth of Portuguese escudos, five thousand of
Venezuelan bolivars, and three thousand each of Greek drachmas,
Brazilian cruzeiros, and Indonesian rupiahs, you'll be living off the
fat of the land before you're one month older. Or, if you're on

Weight Watchers, you can live off the cottage cheese of the land, but please, no more than one piece of toast daily.

One key indicator in foreign currency speculation is the fut. What, you may ask, is the fut?

Open your newspaper, turn to the foreign exchange listing in the financial section, and look where it says "W. Germany (mark):30-day fut, 60-day fut, 90-day fut." Now, you probably think fut is an abbreviation for future, proving once again that you haven't the brains you were born with. A fut is a brass token used to get on a German bus. There are three futs to a mark, except Sundays, when you get to ride free if you show your *Alter Cocker* (senior citizen) pass. One fut will get you from Berlin to Munich, two from Berlin to Dresden, and three from Berlin to Stuttgart. You can also take an airplane from Stuttgart to Dresden using a flying fut, but most unscheduled airlines don't give flying futs, and you generally have to bribe the pilot.

Most people use their futs for transportation, but some sophisticated speculators play the "fut float," which is the time it takes between the moment riders put their futs in the coin box and the moment the bus pulls into the garage. By using your fut to buy Turkish lire during that period of time, then selling them off for South African escudos, you can make a tidy profit. But it calls for nerves of steel, and it helps if you have an edge, like knowing if the bus driver is a speed demon or a slowpoke. Some fut fetishists study bus schedules like racing forms!

God help you if you get caught in a short position with your futs out, so if this game is too nervewracking for you, stick to more humdrum currency exchanges, like how many dimes in a dollar, how many nickels in a quarter, etc.

Collectibles

One of the most interesting forms of economic hedge is the collectible. The rewards to be reaped for accurately guessing which worthless object will be invaluable five, ten, or fifty years from now are incredible. On the other hand, many an investor's ship has been wrecked on the shoals of collectibles after being crushed between the

Scylla of inventory expenses and the Charybdis of fickle public taste. Wasn't that a honey of an extended metaphor?

Millions have been made on paintings, stamps, furniture, coins, and porcelains, to name a few, by men and women who bought and sold at the right time. But they had an uncanny sense of what was going to become hot, and when. I can predict with complete certainty, for instance, that one of the most valuable collectibles of the coming decade will be Rembrandt's "Aristotle Contemplating the Bust of Homer." It's true that this picture is on exhibit under guard at New York's Metropolitan Museum, but if there's any way you can remove it and hold onto it for a few years, the profit could well nigh be astonishing.

We know that certain collectibles, like plastic drinking straws, aluminum ashtrays stamped with the Empire State Building, and straw-and-seashell Puerto Rican handbags, have been steadily rising in value, but only to a degree sufficient to keep up with inflation. That Empire State Building ashtray could be bought in Times Square for one dollar five years ago; now it sells for a dollar fifty, but so what? You also have a storage problem. Between warehousing, insurance, and carrying charges, if you keep two million plastic straws for ten years hoping they'll become collectors' items, you'll actually lose money, even if your prices keep up with inflation.

One way to increase the value of collectibles is to destroy most of them to make the remaining ones more valuable. One collector of Red Cross doughnuts, figuring people would be desperate for them when the world ended, destroyed all but six of his stock of 300,000 and was able to sell them at Sotheby Parke Bernet recently for $75,000 apiece, except for the honey-dipped which fetched $85,000.

Another way to inflate the price of a collectible is to flaw it in some way. Postage stamps appreciate wildly when it is discovered that a printer goofed and printed an airplane upside down or misspelled the queen's name. You can do the same for your collectible. One shrewd collector of Puerto Rican straw-and-shell handbags ripped out the stitched slogan "Puerto Rico Beckons You" and had his entire stock of 200,000 bags resewn with "Puerto Rico Beckons Yog." He sold them out overnight at three times his cost.

So—what do you think is going to be the Picasso lithograph or

Tiffany lamp of tomorrow? Whatever it is, collect it. What's that you say? You collect Polish jokes? Okay, let's hear one.

Q. How did the Pole burn his ear?

A. He was ironing when the phone rang.

New Careers in Armageddon

> *"The shocking thing is that most of the looters*
> *didn't feel they were doing anything wrong. And*
> *many of the so-called upright citizens were actu-*
> *ally urging teenagers on, asking to 'get me one of*
> *those,' or 'I could sure use a new bed.'"*
> —HOWARD J. RUFF, *How to Prosper*
> *During the Coming Bad Years*

Quickly now, without thinking: what's the first thing you would do if you learned the end of the world was imminent? You *would?* You really would?

Well, my friend, except for a few weirdos like you, most people would flee. This has been scientifically demonstrated by Russian researchers in the so-called Great Vladivostok Fleeing Experiment, which you can reproduce with equally tragic results in your own home.

Armed with the knowledge that the Great Day of Reckoning is coming, career-minded individuals can go into fields of endeavor that will yield tremendous satisfaction, to say nothing of profits, in the mounting panic of the coming lousy years. Indeed, thousands of career opportunities are just opening up in such fields as Fleeing, Hiding, Doomsday Insurance, and End of the World Prophecy. Let's look at these in detail.

Fleeing

The first thing you must ask yourself is, What will people need when they learn the end of the world is nigh and they decide to get away from it all?

Right off, we know they will need luggage. Unless they are

47

particularly crazed with panic, they are going to stop to ask themselves, "What do I need to take with me in my flight to safety? And what can I carry it in?"

There is only so much you can carry in a Macy's paper shopping bag. Macy's shopping bags are fine for hauling home Christmas gifts, but they have no compartments, are fragile in inclement weather, and don't really evince status.

You should therefore start a line of evacuation luggage. The better models will be made of leather with hidden pockets and false bottoms for valuables, but as not everyone can afford leather, you might produce cheaper models along the lines of those long poles and handkerchiefs commonly carried by victims of Communist invasions. These are useful for short-to-medium-range evacuations, but for anything over twenty miles they are unreliable: shirts get wrinkled, trousers crushed, and your mouthwash bottle breaks and spills over your krugerrand collection—it's a real mess.

So stick to leather, vinyl, or canvas. For a few hundred dollars extra you can provide personalized valises and suitcases with monograms in tin leaf (gold leaf is out of the question). The name tag will provide a bit of a problem, as you can't state either your home address (you're fleeing from that one, remember?) or the one you're fleeing to (because you don't know it). And where the tag says, "In case of emergency notify _____"? it's hard to know what goes on that line. Everyone you can think of will be fleeing, too.

Next, people will need fast, reliable transportation, and there are high profits to be made for anyone who anticipates this vital need. Yes, I hear you saying (that *is* you—I'd know that stutter anywhere), but what am I supposed to do, buy a fleet of airplanes or cars? Buy a railroad? These things cost a lot of money (this is still you speaking)! I can't raise that kind of capital.

That's where you're wrong (this is me speaking now). You don't have to buy a single plane, train, boat, or car in order to make a killing in evacuation transportation. How often have you read that planes have been grounded for want of a part that cost a nickel? Did you ever wonder what that part was? Well, now is the time to find out and buy every one you can lay your hands on. Same goes for car parts, boat parts, etc. Corner the market on vital parts worth a

MAKE A KILLING IN EVACUATIONS
Corner the market in vital auto parts and sell them at a premium
to drivers of stalled cars.

nickel, then just sit back and wait for the stampede of desperate evacuees. When the lines of stalled cars and grounded planes begin to stretch from here to kingdom come, *you're* going to show up with your bagful of vital parts worth a nickel. Of course, they may be *worth* a nickel, but you're going to be selling them for four thousand dollars apiece, right? You're going to be selling them for as much as the *traffic* will bear!

And—if business is a little slow, my newsletter will show you how to damage those parts imperceptibly but irreparably so that they fail after a few hours and people have to come to you for replacements.

While these evacuees are lined up bumper to bumper, they'll need something to read. You'll be ready for them with your line of paperback novels sold car to car. Never has the phrase "escape literature" been more appropriate.

What sort of thing does someone read while hung up in doomsday traffic waiting for some vital part worth a nickel? A recent poll of drivers and passengers stalled on Ventura Boulevard during a recent mock invasion of Los Angeles from outer space revealed that people turn to inspirational classics in time of need. Among the favorites mentioned by stranded Angelenos were:

> *Brenda Starr, Reporter* by Dale Messick
> *Peanuts* by Charles Schulz
> *The Adventures of Pogo* by Walt Kelly
> *Dennis the Menace* by Hank Ketchum
> *Li'l Abner* by Al Capp.

Stock up now at the nearest bookstore.

If you're clever in the kitchen, you might want to go into picnic lunches and other food concessions for evacuees. You can bet that after trudging on hot dusty roads all day, bumped and pummeled by hysterical fugitives and beaten and robbed by unscrupulous highwaymen, these folks will have worked up a hearty appetite.

What do evacuees like to eat? Another recent survey was conducted of people fleeing the site of a railroad accident where tank cars were leaking fluorine gas. It was not always easy to understand them, gagging and sputtering as they were, but the essence of what they said is that most fleeing people crave simple but wholesome foods that can be eaten without implements. It should not be spicy. So the ideal evacuation lunch box might consist of a ham-and-cheese sandwich on white bread with a piece of fruit. Obviously, simplicity is the byword here—fleeing people have a lot on their minds and can't be bothered by vexing questions like whole wheat or rye, American cheese or Swiss, boiled ham or baked, to say nothing of having to choose among snails in garlic butter, roast Long Island duckling with plum sauce, or terrine of pork with *cornichons*.

Naturally, if you want to slip in something piquant like curry or chili, or a salty side order of french fries, or some thirst-inducing ice cream, your profits will rise dramatically. Why? Because a hundred yards down the road, you're going to have a soft-drink concession at prices nothing short of outrageous.

At the same roadside rest, the enterprising concessionaire may want to stock such necessary items as maps, bibles, compasses, tools, and weapons. And don't forget the most important thing: souvenirs.

My brother-in-law has been test-marketing a line of doomsday souvenirs that should go over real big, such as buttons that say, "Kiss me, I'm bankrupt," "Buddy can you spare twenty thou," "Prepare to meet thy creditor," "Karl Marx was wrong," "Chicken Little was right," "Barter is smarter," "Bring back Milton Friedman," "Support your local looters," and "Remember the Federal Reserve system."

Other souvenirs might be a piece of a teller's window from a recently ransacked bank, Chrysler Corporation stock certificates, and plasticized newspaper clippings about the good old days of low interest rates. You might try selling paper dollars as collectors' items at three for a thousand dollars, as opposed to their monetary value of one thousand for three dollars. Doomsday greeting cards should go over big, with humorous sayings accompanying pictures of Pompeii, Johnstown, Krakatoa, Nagasaki, etc. One item that test-marketed real well was my cousin Sylvia's Little Lazarus Resurrection Kit. Consisting of a cave, a shroud, a heavy rock, a brilliant aura, and a bottle of Gatorade, it should jump off your shelves even when sales of other souvenirs are moving sluggishly.

Going Into Hiding

Above all, people are going to need places to hide, and you should seriously consider getting into the hiding industry. Now in its infancy, hiding is one of the fastest-growing branches of the leisure field, with a billion dollars in gross bookings reported in the second quarter of 1979, as opposed to $15.75 in the same quarter of 1978. Projections for the 1980s suggest a sky's-the-limit future for hiding, so there's lots of room for go-getters.

Where will people want to be when the world ends? In preparing this book, I did a number of man-in-the-street interviews. The responses were most revealing. Here, verbatim (but with taxi drivers' oaths omitted), are some typical man-in-the-street answers to the question, Where will you want to be when the world ends?

> At the foot of Mount Sinai to pray
>
> At the top of Mount Sinai to jump
>
> In a library snuggled up with the new Robert Ludlum
>
> Anywhere snuggled up with anyone
>
> In Neiman-Marcus to spend
>
> In Sears to save
>
> In a Holiday Inn to sleep
>
> In a Howard Johnson's to eat
>
> In an Exxon station to pee

By shrewdly but discreetly buying up properties where people will want to hide, you can be ready to service all these leaping, sleeping, fleeing, peeing, reading, breeding people. Naturally, there will be obstacles to purchasing Neiman-Marcus or Holiday Inn, but you never know till you try. Call Neiman-Marcus and sound them out! Call Sears! Call Mount Sinai! All you need is *one* of these properties. I'll bet Howard Johnson's would sell to you if you asked them nicely.

The question, where are the best places to hide from the end of the world? comes up quite often. Naturally, it depends on what, exactly, you're hiding from. If it's from war, you'll want one kind of place, if it's from disease or famine, you'll want another. A good place to hide from war, for instance, is Switzerland; from famine, Miami Beach; from pestilence, Miami Beach.

Not long ago, Marinière and Ravigote, a team of prison guards wit sociology degrees, performed an experiment that shed much light on the question of hiding places. They intentionally permitted twenty-five hard-bitten murderers, thieves, and rapists to escape from the psycho ward of a major East Coast prison. Mariniere and Ravigote then followed them, taking notes on their movements. Unfortunately, both observers were quickly detected in their Groucho false noses, moustaches, and eyeglasses and were dismembered by the subjects and sent back in six separate valises, so our data on the experiment are, not surprisingly, sketchy. However, in the thirty-eight-state manhunt that ensued, resulting in the recapture of sixteen of the twenty-five, officials were able to learn the following from the debriefings:

Fourteen escapees crossed into Canada, not so much for safety as because they'd heard about a terrific new restaurant in Montreal specializing in *truite amandine,* and they hadn't had a good *truite amandine* in five to thirty years. They were quickly rounded up by the Mounties and were generally in agreement that the trout was not fresh.

Five escapees fled to Trenton, New Jersey, figuring quite rightly that it's impossible to find Trenton, New Jersey. They are there to this day, sending taunting letters to prison officials.

Two headed for the nearest island they could think of. It happened to be Coney, and they were captured after a brief struggle while stepping off the Octopus.

Four headed for Hollywood, where they started their own studio. Their first film is scheduled for general release at 800 neighborhood theaters in April. Please consult your newspaper for times.

Anyone with information concerning the whereabouts of Johnny ("Rusty Scimitar") McGinty, Max ("Two-thirds of a Face") Klieglight, and Alphonse Payton Morgan-Biddle-Mellon III ("The Hobnail Boot Rapist"), report to the FBI—there's a ten-thousand-dollar reward. And while we're at it, anyone knowing the whereabouts of my brother-in-law Murray, give me a call—he owes me five hundred dollars.

Now that we know more about the sorts of places people will want to flee to when civilization as we know it collapses, you might seriously consider starting a hiding agency. You can design it along the lines of the one run by my cousin Betty Ann. Betty Ann's agency is structured to cater to the needs of fleeing people of either modest or unlimited budgets. If, for instance, you can't afford the deluxe box lunch for $650, she'll sell you one with plainer fare for $395. The difference is mainly white bread vs. seeded roll, so I think you're wise going economy class anyway.

Among the services performed by a hiding agency are:

1. *Group Evacuations.* If you have a group of twenty-five or more people fleeing to the same place—say, your bridge club contemplates stampeding in blind panic to Ketchikan, Alaska—a hiding agency will arrange a package stampede, including breakfasts and dinners (lunches and bedtime snacks optional) and a book of special certificates entitling you to a free Tom Collins and a 10 percent army-blanket discount when you arrive. As in most charter bookings, you don't even have to belong to a bona fide club or group to qualify for the package rate; you merely have to have something in common with your fellow evacuees, such as abject terror. You may cancel with full refund up to twenty-four hours before the blind panic is scheduled to begin, and, of course, if doomsday is for any reason canceled or postponed, your fees will be applied toward a rescheduled one.

2. *Hideaways.* A hiding agency should, of course, provide clients with places to hide, such as caves, sewer systems, bomb shelters, abandoned houses, sidetracked boxcars, and storm cellars. These would be available on short- or long-term basis, furnished or unfurnished, frills or no-frills.

Short- and long-term leases are based on the E.T.A., or Estimated Time of Apocalypse, with a minimum E.T.A. of one week. As might be expected, the elaborateness of the furnishings is directly related to the length of the lease. If doomsday is expected within one week, you're lucky to find a chamber pot in your hiding place. If, on the other hand, the end of the world isn't predicted until six months

NEW CAREERS IN ARMAGEDDON
Run a luxury condo colony for wealthy evacuees. Arrange for package
stampedes, offer ten percent army blanket discounts.

or longer, you can find a cave or sewer furnished to a faretheewell. Betty Ann's "Bitter End Hide-in Condo," for instance, offers a hideaway complete with highly embellished ormolu countdown clocks, chased-steel gun emplacements, and antique pillboxes with cyanide tablets.

3. *Other Services.* As most fleeing people will have little furniture, you can run a profitable side business by buying up their furniture from them cheaply when they start their flight, then selling it back to them for a lot of money when they arrive at their destinations.

Your agency can arrange for sublessees if desired by tenants. Often, a cavern or boxcar will be too large for a small family, and agents can provide them with space sharers to help out with the costs and chores. Here is where a good agent can prove invaluable, for if you get just any old sublessee, things (which are after all uncomfortable enough) can get awfully unpleasant. You don't, while resignedly saying your prayers during the waning moments of life on this planet, want some panic-stricken idiot running around in circles blubbering, "I don't want to die, I don't want to die!" Your agency

will have screened and tested applicants for apocalybility and made
sure that they, like you, are the sort who will succumb with quiet
acceptance, if not a broad grin.

Many hiding agencies provide limited legal services, such as
witnessing wills, but don't expect more than that. Nor should your
clients expect your agency to exchange or lend money, undertake
repairs or improvements on the property, furnish food, or perform
funeral or wedding services unless specified in the agreement.
Clients should read their contracts carefully and bear in mind that,
once the world ends, it will be difficult to get a breach of contract
suit heard in most courts.

Chaos

In the twilight period between the time we learn the world is
ending and the actual event, there is going to be untold chaos. After
all, when people know that life on earth is soon to be terminated,
they get very cranky. Anyone with the faintest entrepreneurial
ambitions will recognize the huge profits to be made in the so-called
chaos market. Consider going into this lucrative field.

A shrewd chaos engineer (as they are coming to be called) can run
up a big score by stockpiling material required for proper plunder-
ing, pillaging, rape, and mayhem. Guns and knives, blunt instru-
ments, and more exotic weapons like sharpened motorcycle chains
will be much in demand. A clever chaos engineer will be right there
with his arsenal of violent implements quietly accumulated during
the buildup of the crisis.

One way to make people buy your wares is to spring upon them a
variation of the "Three-Day Test" devised by the editor of one
survival newsletter. "Without further discussion," he recommends,
"you should get up and turn off the utility services coming into your
home. This would include electricity, natural gas, and water." See if
your family is able to survive an emergency sans water, heat,
telephone, or, worst of all, television. The implication is that by the
end of three days, your family will be at each other's throats.

Okay. Having done that, you're now ready for the big test.
Without further discussion, get up and turn off the utility services
coming into your city. Set up your weapons mart in a convenient

location, sit back, and prepare for the biggest rush of business since the opening of the Oklahoma Territories to settlers.

If this career appeals to you, it's not too soon to begin your work. Start by making maps of jewelry, food, appliance, and other stores in your neighborhood, to sell to looters. Study the newspapers for information about upcoming riots. Tune your radio to emergency channels. Learn to distinguish among siren signals (three longs and a short mean the Dow Jones Average dropped twenty points; two shorts and two longs mean your city's municipal bonds have been downrated from AAA to A, etc.). Manufacture a line of canvas loot bags with your firm name on them or clever slogans like, "I got my diamonds from Tiffany" or "Smash-and-grabbed from Macy's window." Publish directories of plate-glass windows, public statues, and art collections for defacing and desecration by vandals. You might, as an inducement, offer free spray-paint cans to the first hundred purchasers of these directories. Start a gunnery range in the recreation room of your nearest Knights of Columbus meeting hall. Invite Rhodesian mercenaries to lecture your bridge club.

Profits in Prophets

One revered occupation that is coming back into vogue is doomsday prophecy, and it provides unlimited career opportunities for someone going into business for himself. Start out as a prophet or soothsayer; then, when you've gained a little experience, start your own doomsday lecture circuit.

How to become a prophet? The best way is to observe the professionals at work. Watch how they build confidence with surefire predictions like, "There will be a sharp surge," or, "Look for a deceleration," or, "Unemployment is a realistic possibility." Once these predictions are fulfilled, they hire a press agent to send releases to *Time, Newsweek,* and other such magazines, saying, "Six months ago, Professor Alphonse Schrecklich said there was going to be a sharp surge, and he was ignored. Now that we have had a sharp surge, people are beginning to listen."

Once you get your name in the papers, you must follow up with more specific predictions: "There will be a sharp surge in the next six months." It helps if you can give a memorable, bouncy title to your brand of prophecy, such as "Surgism," and organize disciples into the Surgism School. If you can locate the school in a specific locale like a university and get a snappy name for your outfit, so much the better—like Schrecklich's Brain Trust, or the Juilliard School of Music Surgism Bunch.

Soon you'll be on a roll, with sharp surges manifesting themselves everywhere in the economy. From time to time there may be no sharp surges. You can turn these reversals to your advantage: "The economy is quietly gathering itself for another sharp surge," you can say; or, "Key sectors are recovering from the recent sharp surge."

Now all you have to do is wait for the call from the White House telling you your philosophy has been adopted by the President, and how would you like to work for the government? Here comes the sharp surge in *your* fortunes, because you will now be able to shift your approach from garden-variety prophecy to the self-fulfilling kind. The President will tell you, "We need a sharp surge, and we need it soon." By recommending a few billion spent here or there, or raising interest by a point or two, you can make the economy surge sharply through a hoop.

After the government has been roundly clobbered in the next election, you'll be at loose ends for a while. Keep your press agent; you'll need him to send out releases saying, "The President failed to heed Schrecklich's advice," and, "The Cabinet veered from the orthodox line." Before long you'll be more popular than ever, and you can start saying sooth in other areas. "There will be a sharp surge in immorality," or, "There will be a sharp surge in religious sentiment." Get yourself styled "The Grand Old Man of Surges," or "Mister Surge Himself," or "The Hoary-Headed Prophet of the Grand Concourse." Soon you will be revered.

And that's when you predict the end of the world.

Never forget the first rule of doomsday prophecy: Keep It Vague. Learn to speak in Sybillene circumlocutions, like, "What's gonna be is gonna be." Such is the stock-in-trade of the successful prophet.

The second rule is, Keep a Hereford cow and wait for her to say something in Yiddish. Remember about Hereford cows from the beginning of the book? No? Are you reading this book or just looking at the pictures? I said that just before the world ends,

Hereford cattle begin talking Yiddish. So—you keep a cow and bone up on your Yiddish. Don't confuse it with Afrikaans; more than one linguist has fallen into that error. When you hear that cow uttering the language of the Diaspora, you get up on that pulpit and start doomsaying like it was going out of style, which I suppose it will be, at that point.

You can now send your disciples out on tour. Organize a doomsday lecture circuit and watch the commissions roll in. Where do you get these prophets? In other countries. That's because prophets are without honor in their own countries, so they go to other people's. Just look there.

Your prophets must be prepared to take a certain amount of abuse. Skeptics are always testing prophets in the hopes of separating true ones from false. They dunk them, stone them, burn them, torture them, and so on. Pick your prophets carefully. They should be determined and have thick skins. If they do suffer or splutter when dunked or say "Ouch!" when burned at the stake, or even if they are forced to renounce, they should bear in mind that on the day of reckoning, they'll have the last laugh.

Miscellaneous Careers

As prophecy may not be to everybody's liking, there are countless other fields to enter. If you like to work outdoors, consider becoming a landscape artist for bomb shelters and bunkers. Unsightly dirt mounds covering underground hideouts must be covered with sod and planted with azaleas and other shrubs. Ivy can be trained to grow over propane tanks and sniper emplacements. Mine fields should be seeded for marigolds, morning glories, and begonias.

Marksmanship instructors will be in great demand, particularly for children who have never handled guns. Karate, judo, and hand-to-hand combat for senior citizens will be popular courses. Anyone with expertise in boobytrapping, explosives, ammunition, pyrotechnics, and similar topics should find all the work he can handle.

The radical changes in eating habits occasioned by predoomsday scarcity should provide lots of employment for chefs, short-order chefs in particular, as most orders will be quite short, indeed—it will mainly be a matter of adding water. Still, as some people add water better than others, there will be plenty of upward mobility for the imaginative cook.

In fact, there will be so many alterations in life-styles that just about anyone capable of putting two words together will be able to make it as a journalist. Magazines will spring up like mushrooms, carrying such articles as "How to Dress for a Food Riot," "How to Prepare Guest Lists for Bunkers," "Proper Makeup for Sieges," "What to Do If Your Doctor Is Dead," "Don't Throw Out That Garbage—Use It!", "Do-it-yourself Burial Services"—the possibilities are endless.

Have you considered a career in the insurance field? It may be the hottest career of all in the coming years. Policies are being redesigned even as I write this, to cover losses incurred by the end of the world. In fact, though few people know it, some insurance companies are already offering doomsday insurance, and the premiums aren't that high. Nevertheless, it pays to shop around for the best deal. Mutual of Flatbush's "Dies Irae" rider, for instance, provides the following for a premium of only a few hundred dollars a day:

> If you are trampled to death on the Throg's Neck Bridge, a $50,000 lump-sum benefit is awarded to your next of kin, unless that next of kin has been trampled with you, in which case it goes to your podiatrist.

> If you lose a hand as a result of an unsuccessful attempt to loot a bank cash machine: $25,000.

> For injuries sustained from being struck on the head by a falling bankrupt: $10,000.

> In the event you are wiped out by the collapse of the economy, your insurer will issue you a Starting Over kit, consisting of a five-dollar bill, a slightly used overcoat, a lump of sourdough, and a letter of introduction to the foreman of a Cuban cane sugar factory.

You may want to go into the doomsday insurance business. The field is wide open. Consider the actuarial tables: it is 100 percent guaranteed that the world will end, sooner or later. As Damon Runyon said, "Life is three to two against." With odds like that, you've got to do OK.

The Scarcity Investment Plan

"There is nothing so disastrous as a rational investment policy in an irrational world."
—JOHN MAYNARD KEYNES, economist

If you're going to make it big in the coming cataclysm, you'll have to figure out what's going to be scarce, buy it up, hold onto it, and sell it for lots of money when hard times hit.

Over the last few years since I declared myself the unchallenged king of pessimism, I have developed a surefire system of doping winners in the investment field. It's called the Scarcity Investment Plan, and readers of my newsletter who have scrupulously followed the plan report immeasurable profits. Using the Gatti-Cassaza Price-Profit Index (adjusted for effeminate Comanches), we find that if, in 1960, you had $1,000 to invest, here is how much money you'd have earned today by investing in . . .

New York Stock Exchange 50 Top Industrials . . . $2,500.00

Corn Exchange 3,000.00

Witty Exchange. 5,000.00

Meaningful Exchange 6,500.00

Prisoner Exchange 50,000.00

Gold bullion 75,000.00

Gold Circle Pins 80,000.00

Picassos (Blue Period) 100,000.00

Picassos (Recovery Period). 250,000.00

Heroin	300,000.00
"The Fantasticks"	350,000.00
Only one "Fantastick"	25,000.00
Copper Hydrosulphate (use in making duck wings)	159.75
Land Cameras	800,000.00
Air Cameras	750,000.00
New York Municipal Bonds	(2,500,000.00)
Sixth at Pimlico	$5.40, 4.50, and $2.10
Scarcity Investment Plan	116,500,486.98

Why has the Scarcity Investment Plan been so phenomenally successful? Because it anticipated products and services people would desperately need in the 1970s. Some of the products were: roller-skate keys, gas-tank locks, and dog-poop bags. Among the services that sharply escalated in value were: closing hospitals, adjusting gas station pump meters, and setting fires for insurance.

Let's take a look at just one product which, had you taken my advice a decade ago, would have made you stinking rich today. In 1970, Hiram Lovett, a small New Jersey businessman, had recently lost his shirt. (He thought he'd left it in the third drawer of his dresser, but his wife said he never picked up the Chinese laundry.) Hiram read an article in my newsletter about how cities were passing stricter laws about dog doody. He immediately perceived a wave of the future and borrowed ten thousand dollars from a Mafia loan shark to start the Hiram Lovett Poop and Food Storage Bag Company. This name he shortened to the Hiram Lovett Poop Bag after Food and Drug Administration investigators cited possible sanitary code violations.

His firm skyrocketed into *Fortune* magazine's 500 Most Tedious Industrial Firms. It was capitalized at close to one million dollars, or, if you don't count the interest on his Mafia loan, $14.50. Had you taken the advice proffered in our newsletter at that time and bought Lovett's Poop Bags, you'd be riding high, for his poop bags have split fifteen times since the original stock offering.

Now—what consumer products or services of the future will be in the same urgent demand that Lovett's are today?

Consider, for instance, how many people will be declaring bankruptcy. You should be able to cash in on this upswing by anticipating the needs of bankrupts. They'll want cardboard to line their shoes with, Valium, and Chapter XI legal forms. There'll be a heavy demand for gaily striped canvas to replace the awnings through which all those despairing people are going to plummet when they jump out of windows.

You'll also need witnesses. From all indications, this nation is rapidly running out of them. To prove this, next time you come to an intersection in your car, run over some little old man and keep driving. You'll never hear from a soul. That's because of a paucity in the supply of witnesses.

The moment the Apocalypse is announced, you're going to see a flood of legal paper—not merely bankruptcy applications, but wills, deeds, gifts, bills of sale, and receipts. Who's going to witness all those signatures? You won't be able to haul people in from the streets—have you seen what's going on in those streets? You'll need professional witnesses to sign their names beside yours on all those legal documents.

Take what happened to my friend Chauncey Inglenook. In a recent calamity, a flash flood in a dry gulch in Arizona, Inglenook decided to sell off some of his bottomland because he knew it would never again be seen by human eyes. In the mounting hysteria (people were mounting as far as the eye could see), he managed to find a buyer and gave him a terrific price. With water pouring into Inglenook's den, they signed the papers. Then the buyer said, "We should have someone to witness our signatures."

Inglenook scoffed, but the man insisted. They ran to the door of their mobile home. They saw nothing but water, flotsam and jetsam, and an occasional drowned cow. At length, a soy sauce salesman washed up against the door, and they begged him to witness their signatures, but he wanted too much money, and they had to break his fingers and kick him back into the roiling waters. Thus, for want of a witness, Inglenook lost a sale. In his case it turned out to be fortunate, because the bottomland happened to be the site of Phoenix. But it could have been a catastrophe.

The moral of this story is, witnesses are going to be the dog-poop bags of the 1980s. If you buy them up now when they're still cheap, hold them off the market until doomsday, then release them slowly, you'll make a mogul's fortune.

Essential to the success of the Scarcity Investment Plan is knowing not only what is going to be scarce, but what is going to be abundant as well. There are many commodities whose longevity makes them worthless in a world that will not be a world a few months from now. Take kosher salt. How long have you had that box of it? Five years, and you still have all but half an ounce of it. Same with Angostura bitters. How about pear brandy? Marjoram? When was the last time you used a recipe calling for marjoram? Meanwhile, these things are taking up valuable shelf space that should be devoted to items with quick turnover potential. Get rid of them. How? Try putting an ad in the paper. People will buy anything from ads in the paper. "Kosher salt, Angostura bitters, pear brandy, marjoram, forced to sell, moving to new location, will sacrifice, best offer, principals only," etc. You'll find someone, believe me. (For maximum exposure, put an ad in our newsletter. Our rates are best of any in the scare-rag field. Speak to my Aunt Hilda, our advertising manager, about our terrific introductory rates.)

With severe energy shortages besetting the world, many electric gadgets, now considered the latest thing, will be prohibitively expensive to run. Popcorn poppers, bun warmers, Frybabies and Big Macs, electric woks and crockpots, food processors, microwave ovens, and trash compactors will become as obsolete as smithies' anvils.

Anything with a lifetime guarantee is going to be a drug on the market when the end of the world rolls around, and you must create a market for it before it becomes utterly worthless. Mattress pads, car mufflers, three-year leases and thirty-year mortgages, long magazine subscriptions—get rid of them. This can be done by selling short. Anything that looks as if it's going to last more than six months should be sold short.

What exactly is selling short?

Most investors are ignorant about the concept, but it's really quite simple. You borrow whatever it is you want to deal in, sell it, then, when the price drops, you buy it back and return it to the person you borrowed it from. Now let's apply this principle to some commodity you're trying to unload, like mattress pads with lifetime guarantees.

The first and hardest thing to do is borrow them. Say you want to make a deal for ten thousand. Where the hell are you going to borrow ten thousand mattress pads? You'll simply have to go from door to door, ringing bells and asking people if you can borrow their mattress pads for a few weeks. They will, of course, say, "Just what am I supposed to do without a mattress pad for a few weeks?"

Look at them peculiarly. "Do you mean to tell me you still need mattress pads at your age, you big baby? Does your spouse know you're incontinent?" You'll get your mattress pad.

Strip the bed and get out of there. Now what? Well, there is no mattress pad exchange per se, as there is a cocoa or cotton exchange, so you'll have to sell them on your front lawn. Tell everyone who buys them that when the price drops, they should bring them back and you'll buy them. You then take them back to the folks you borrowed them from. Simple enough, right?

Now you know everything about selling short except, how does one tell when the price is going to drop? Well, if you've done your job well, the price will drop, your job being to disseminate ugly rumors about mattress pads, such as that they are the cause of parrot fever.

As selling short is a treacherous game suitable only for the coolest of businessmen (and those with enough room to store ten thousand mattress pads), most of you will want to take the more conventional route of buying commodities cheaply and selling them when the price goes up. I have named many commodities that will appreciate in value, but I have held back on the most important, for I am reluctant to give away in an inexpensive book an idea that I can publish in my newsletter at $200 per subscription. Nevertheless, I am now going to share with you the prediction that is the cornerstone of my Scarcity Investment Plan projections for the 1980s:

By the end of the decade, the world will have run out of meat.

The Decline and Fall of the Cow

Undoubtedly, the reader believes that the coming meat shortage, whose symptoms are already in evidence, is the result of such routine dynamics as increased demand and curtailed supply. You should stop trying to play John Maynard Keynes. The real reason has to do with evolution, for it would appear that our meat-producing livestock are undergoing a rapid genetic change that will render them totally unfit for human consumption within ten years.

Genetic scientists attribute this disturbing phenomenon to the famous Yaphank Flare of 1978, a massive solar excrescence observed by Porfirio Wallbanger of Yaphank, New York, as he was gazing at the sun through binoculars. It home-fried his brains almost instantly, and he had time only to communicate his observation to a friend via CB radio.

Shortly afterwards, scientists detected a solar storm of unprecedented ferocity, and the earth was bombarded for three straight weeks with X-rays, R-rays, PG-rays, cosmic rays, neutrinos, pokerinos, steverinos, quarks, shmarks, and muon pion trions. Fortunately, humans were protected from the gene-destroying effects of this flare by the thin layer of teflon that coats every human epidermis. But as such a layer is absent from the skins of beef cattle, lambs, and pigs, they have developed traits which clearly point to

THE COMING CRISIS IN LIVESTOCK SUPPLY
Due to genetic mutations, beef steers are evolving into a new species
resembling German shorthaired pointers, and pigs into Kodiak bears.

their evolution into inedible creatures. The evidence is indisputable. By the end of the decade, the beef steer will have evolved into an entirely new species resembling German shorthaired pointers, lambs into something along the lines of cassowaries, and pigs into Kodiak bears.

Agricultural and genetic scientists are working feverishly to reverse the trend, but it looks quite grave. An Aberdeen Angus cattle rancher from Newark, New Jersey, recently reported that several of his steers had begun to behave uncharacteristically, racing through meadows baying and yapping, then stopping with nose extended, one forehoof raised, and tail extended. The rancher went on to say that, despite the fact he bagged a brace of partridge and twenty grouse (which the steers retrieved!) he was deeply concerned.

The primary agricultural challenge of the '80s will be to find viable alternatives to beef, lamb, and pork. Some early experiments have proven unsatisfactory. Brisket of German shorthaired pointer, for example, has the texture of a regulation softball sautéed in creosote. Shoulder of Kodiak bear can be compared only to shoulder of Pennsylvania Turnpike in succulence and nutritional value.

Where then will the human race find its substitute for conventional meat?

The Envelope, Please

The answer is: in the human race. It looks as if we're going to be eating people, kids. By the turn of the decade, consumption of human flesh will be as commonplace as the consumption of all-beef patties, lettuce, pickle, and special sauce on a sesame-seed bun is today.

Although the stomach, to say nothing of the duodenum and lower intestine, rebels against this notion, there is a growing population of "homovores" (a word infinitely preferable to "cannibals") who have shed their natural revulsion and are spreading the word as ardently as medieval crusaders—*people are good to eat!* These enthusiasts constitute the nucleus of a market whose growth potential beggars comparision. And by the way, beggars are good to eat, too!

The modern anthropophagical movement may be said to have been born on a cold, lonely mountainside in the Andes mountains, where a planeload of pool sharks was flying from Montevideo to Gary, Indiana, in a Piper Cub to attend the semifinals of the nine-ball regionals, which was to be televised on "Wide World of Sports." What made them think they could possibly clear the Andes or fly 6,000 miles nonstop in a Piper Cub is a mystery that will never be solved, for ten seconds after takeoff the plane struck a tall burro and plunged into a ravine, killing all aboard save Herman ("Six-ball in the Corner Pocket") Kaleeka.

Herman consumed all the beer and pretzels on the plane while waiting to be rescued. Then, as time passed without so much as a hint of a rescue party, he began to eat grass, then snow. Then he ate the fuselage and tail assembly. Finally, looking at the frozen remains of the pilot, a Bolivian midget, he began to get ideas.

Suffering the tortures of the damned, he stared hungrily at that dead midget for three days until he could stand it no longer. At length, the will to live overcame a lifetime of strict religious upbringing, and he succumbed to temptation. Without going into sordid detail, I can report that he ate the part of the pilot that goes over the fence last.

He fell voraciously on the rest of the pilot and the other crew members and passengers, and for weeks dined with a gusto that quite eclipsed the shame we might imagine he felt to do something so antithetical to the good table manners he was taught by his mother, a Seventh Day Adventist, and his father, a Sephardic Jew from Wichita, Kansas. When the rescue party discovered him, he was polishing off the wrist of the first-class cabin hostess. At first the rescuers thought him mad, but he prevailed on them to try just a nibble from the tender part just under the radius bone. They declared the first-class cabin hostess to be first-class indeed, and by the time they returned to civilization (if Gary, Indiana, may be described as civilization), a zealous band of homovores had been born.

Their first task was to find a dependable source of edible humans. Their early efforts, however, were disappointing, if not farcical. First they traveled down to Paraguay, thinking it was Uruguay. After all, both countries end in "guay"—anyone can make that mistake. People are always going to Rumania when they mean to go to Lithuania because they both end in "ania."

Then they got their first break. One of their field researchers reported the existence of huge supplies of edible people on the Anatolian Plain, of a quality ranging from choice to prime. They were cheap and could be moved quickly and in large volume. Deals were struck, a network of middlemen established, and Homovore Associates, a Delaware corporation flying the Liberian flag, was born.

That was 1971. Today, Homovore Associates is a small but rapidly expanding firm with shares available over the counter. Franchising contracts are being let at a brisk pace, and anyone investing in this company today will undoubtedly find himself in the same position in 1990 as those who invested in stone quarries for pyramids found themselves at the end of Egypt's Fourth Dynasty. Although you may obtain a prospectus from your broker, my Uncle Eddie happens to be vice-president in charge of torsos and a 51 percent stockholder, and has kindly permitted me to summarize the offering plan.

Supply of People

Most eating people are grown on the Turkish plain where the dry air, rich soil, and adequate rainfall create conditions for splendid meat. Even traditionally chewy old people are more tender from this region than from others. Turkish-grown people have attractive marbling, good color, and are chemical-free. Eating people are also grown in Southeast Asia but are generally tougher and have an unacceptable amount of toxic chemicals in their flesh, owing to the defoliants used in the recent wars.

It should be stressed that these people are *fresh*. Homovore Associates does not, and will not, desecrate tombs for its supply.

Processing of People

After being harvested, the eating people are transported to Marseilles for processing. In Marseilles, the people are packed and loaded into the holds of ships bound for America. New York is, of course, the principal port of entry, but some people come in via Baltimore and Boston. It is important when buying human to look for the official seal of the port of entry on each package. If you see something like Needles, Arizona, stamped on your package, it is very likely ersatz or adulterated.

Economics of People

Today, even the worst cuts of beef, pork, or lamb sell for no less than $2.39 per pound as this book goes to press. Compare this with human. You can get prime human for $1.89 per pound, boned and dressed, and usually for ten cents less you can get it boned and *un*-dressed (some people buy the dresses to make soup stock).

Of course, some parts are more expensive, such as the tongue and sweetbreads. On the other hand, if you buy humans on the hoof (or, more accurately, on the foot), you can get excellent discounts. Some consumers buy a whole side of person for storage in freezer lockers.

Nutritional Value of People

Human flesh has been demonstrated to be much more nutritional than conventional meats, and, indeed, much higher in nutritional value than any other food except pistachio nuts. One eight-ounce serving of human biceps, for instance, contains all the minimum daily requirements of Niacin; Thiamin; Riboflavin; Vitamins A, B, B1, B-12, C, D, and E; calcium; protein; and traces of Einsteinium, molybdenum, plutonium, and duodenum. One human knuckle is equivalent in nutritional value to three bowls of sour cream and chives.

Sometimes nitrites are added to preserve the shelf life of a human. If you can a person, he'll last indefinitely. Frozen, he can be stored for months. But if you leave a human out on your kitchen counter for any length of time at room temperature, he'll get high and go rotten like anything else.

Types of Human

One question often comes up: do Caucasians taste better than Orientals, or black people better than red?

It would appear that when it comes to taste, people are the same under the skin. There are local variations, of course, as well as subtle differences among nationalities. I personally have an aversion to Arabs, for example, but I dote on Arubans. I had a terrific Aruban just the other night, sweet and succulent as if it had been popped into the oven just moments after I ordered it, and, indeed, that would account for the disappearance of our busboy.

Age is also a factor. As in any other kind of meat, the younger the better. Old people, though tougher, are also cheaper. Very old people can be too tough even for stewing meat, but if you're hard-up and have to eat an old person, pound him with a mallet for half an hour and add a little Adolph. I don't mean Adolph's Meat Tenderizer, I mean Adolph the human. It's amazing what a little Adolph can do for a bad piece of person.

Some Favorite Human Dishes

I have a number of favorite recipes calling for humans. These include Roast Rump of Nova Scotia Tuna Fisherman, Pickled Gums of Australian Sheepherder, and Fried Pippick of Nigerian Cotton Chopper. My very favorite is Braised Ankle of Jordanian Woman, and I'd like to share that recipe with you.

Braised Ankle of Jordanian Woman

1 Jordanian woman	1 banana skin
2 tsp butter or human fat	2 galoshes, left or right, but not both
1 tbsp sugar	3 labels from Wheaties boxes
2 lbs Idaho potatoes	Salt and pepper to taste
1 qt Calvados	Rosemary

Take the Jordanian woman, clean her thoroughly, and separate her ankle from the rest of her. Store the rest in freezer. Fillet the ankle. If you are unsure about how to fillet an ankle, ask your butcher to do it for you.

Braise her in butter or human fat until brown on all sides, add potatoes and galoshes, sauté until someone calls the fire department. Add banana skins, salt and pepper, sugar, and Calvados; cover and simmer over low heat for two hours or until the galoshes fall apart. Add Rosemary—not the spice: *Rosemary*. Just before serving, sprinkle with labels from Wheaties box.

Yield: serves six.

As an investment for the eighties, you couldn't ask for a better buy than Homovore Associates stock. You'll also be easing the apocalypse by promulgating population control. What better way to keep flourishing human populations down than by eating them? Large supplies of people for eating purposes are expected to come onto the market as the recession deepens and large numbers of workers are laid off, and if these supplies run thin, we can comb out our prisons and thin out the welfare rolls.

Humans as food? Don't knock them if you haven't tried them.

The Last Days: A Scenario

"If things work out pretty much as I've presented them in this book, I'll be back in a few years with more—ready to accept your gratitude and applause. You won't have to call me; I'll certainly call you. But if things don't work out, you may have trouble finding me."
—HARRY BROWNE, *New Profits from the Monetary Crisis*

Sometime in the near future, the White House, in accordance with its policy of spending more and more money to stimulate the economy, will make a dramatic announcement: "The drinks are on the government!" Thirsty Americans will flood bars and cocktail lounges in every community in the country, and for weeks we shall see profligacy that makes the Prohibition era look like a communion service. When it is over, barkeeps will send grossly overinflated bills to the Treasury Department, which will have to print a special currency ("wetbacks") to pay them. When this currency proves worthless, the barkeeps will join the tens of millions of drunken revelers wreaking mayhem in the streets.

The President will call on Congress to give him special powers, and they'll pass a law enabling him to levitate, read minds, and bend spoons without touching them. Congress will also authorize him to seize the reins of government dictatorially and suspend civil liberties.

Presently, everything will be regulated. You won't be allowed to drive your car faster than 55 miles per hour. Social Security payments will be deducted from your paycheck. High taxes will be imposed on cigarettes and gasoline. Privacy will be invaded. You'll have to report large racetrack winnings to the Internal Revenue

74

Service. You'll have to pass through security checkpoints at airport boarding gates. The government will become a partner in everything you do, from drilling for oil to hiring and firing employees. They'll penalize you with high income taxes for being single and encourage you with high subsidies for planting cotton.

The citizenry will, of course, rebel, whereupon the President will call out the National Guard. Predictably, the National Guard won't know where to meet and will end up assembled at the post office in the belief there is a strike there. The National Guard will sort the mails, and the postal system will become utterly chaotic, with first-class letters taking five or six days to reach destinations in the same zip code from which they were sent. At length, there will be anarchy in the streets.

In the ensuing paralysis, Canada will liberate Poughkeepsie, New York, toward which it has always harbored territorial ambitions, and Mexico will try to seize Lubbock, Texas, which called Mexico a dirty name in 1844. Other nations will get into the act. Chad will declare war on the Cameroons for cheating in a pinochle game, the OPEC nations will kick Kuwait out of the confederation for getting one of the Seven Sisters pregnant, and West Germany will dock Italy for being three weeks late.

Finally, under tremendous pressure to act (he'd played the Prince in his high school's production of *Sleeping Beauty)*, the President will invoke his dreaded ultimate power: he will press the button that will reduce the planet to a cinder.

Fortunately for the planet, the people who installed the nuclear black box in his office inadvertently screwed up the wiring. The red wire which was supposed to be attached to terminal A went to terminal B, and the yellow wire that was supposed to go to terminal B went to terminal A. As a result, he will merely ring the kitchen, and the night caretaker will send up a glass of Fresca. The Russians, however, will nevertheless take this to be a hostile gesture and launch a rain of missiles, and believe me, there'll be no confusion in *their* minds between which button gets the Fresca and which button wipes out America. Luckily for us, our second-strike capability is sufficient not only to blast Russia off the map but to redress our grievances with all the other nations that crossed us at one time or another. *"That's* for impressing our sailors in 1751!" we can say to

England; "Take *that* for dumping cheap shoes on us!" we can say to Italy; "This one's for not letting us fish in your territorial waters for sardines!" we can say to Norway.

And that will be it for the world, folks.

As this scenario, or one of those described earlier, unfolds, the human race will begin its last roller boogie on earth. Those of you who have studied this book devoutly will have reaped your unconscionable profits and repaired to your stately mansions to witness, in total leisure and luxury, the final death jerks of your fellow humans. Those not so fortunate will, after a brief period of futile hyperactivity, collapse, shaking a fist at the heavens or at the taxi that missed you by this much as you were crossing Forty-third Street.

Most of us will go to our doom in much the same way we lived our lives—ignorant, afraid, penniless, and never having gotten into the King Tut Exhibition. Indeed, most of us will go to our doom wearing the same clothes we had on when we got home from work.

Whether or not we are winners in the great Game of Life, the end will come for us all the same way. The question we must ask ourselves is, will we succumb with style, grace, and dignity? Or will we be cowardly and boorish?

All those in favor of style, grace, and dignity, raise your right hand.

All those in favor of being cowardly and boorish?

I see.

Going Out in Style

For the two or three of you who voted for the former, here are some things to think about.

1. *What should one wear to Doomsday?*

For men, dress should be on the casual side—sports jacket with open-collared shirt, comfortable slacks, loafers or dress shoes. Track shoes, sandals, blue jeans, workshirts or Hawaiian shirts and the like are definitely to be discouraged.

For women, skirt and blouse or sweater, blazer, flats or open-toed sandals. No shorts or pedal pushers, nothing too tight or revealing. Hats are optional for either sex. Jewelry is out.

2. *Should one pack a suitcase for Doomsday?*

WHAT SHOULD ONE WEAR TO DOOMSDAY?
Casual is best, but nothing too tight or revealing. Expensive jewelry is out:
you can't take it with you.

When in doubt, a good rule to remember is, You can't take it with you, but if you simply have to bring something, then pack a small valise containing a robe, some jammies or a nightie, a few changes of underwear, some extra pairs of slacks, skirts, shirts, sweaters, and jackets. Maybe a pair of sneakers in case there's tennis, and a pair of trunks or a bikini if you think they'll have a pool. A shaving kit or cosmetic bag wouldn't hurt, and it's probably a good idea to bring a few things to bribe the natives with, like nylon stockings, chocolates, and junk jewelry or other shiny objects. And don't leave home without your American Express card.

Bring some aspirin and instant coffee, and maybe something to treat snakebite, narcolepsy, and pellagra. A paperback or two, a pair of sunglasses, and a carton of cigarettes. Cash? Maybe fifty dollars, plus a few dollars extra in quarters for tipping.

3. *What should one eat before the end of the world?*

It's probably best, before Doomsday, to have a light dinner, nothing too salty, definitely no Chinese. Soup and salad or quiche is ideal.

Some people, however, feel, what the hell, let's blow everything on a banquet. We only live once, let's go to hell with ourselves, etc. Not long ago I surveyed a dozen *cordon bleu* chefs and asked them what dishes they would serve if their next meal were their last on earth.

Most of them came up with the usual boring fare—*fillet of sole Walewska, tournedos Rossini, escalope de veau morillons, canard rôti au cassis, venison cutlet with sauce poivrade*—nothing you can't get on any weekday night at Troigros or Lutèce.

Only one chef, Jacques Zerippere, came up with a meal so unique that we present it here in full:

JACQUES ZERIPPERE'S LAST SUPPER

Unleavened Bread

Roasted lamb shank

Roasted egg

Saltwater

Bitter herbs

Charoscs (apple, nuts, cinnamon, and wine mixture)

Parsley, lettuce, or watercress

Zerippere's menu may not be as sumptuous as Scampi Posillipo or Lapin aux Pruneaux, but it possesses that classic simplicity and elegance that are the signs of a *maître de cuisine* and will help create a mood of serenity and acceptance when the last trumpet sounds.

4. *Will a last trumpet really sound, or will there just be this terrific explosion?*

There will just be this terrific explosion. Why do you have to take everything I say literally?

5. *What if Doomsday falls on Super Bowl Sunday or the day when I have tickets for Led Zeppelin?*

Tough.

6. *What loose ends should I tie up before the end of the world?*

There are numerous things you should remember to do before the world ends. Here are a number of them:

> Pick up your film, your dry cleaning, and your Chinese laundry.

> Get your shoes back from the repair shop. Don't make any puns about "soles" and "last"—no one will find them funny.

> Cancel your subscription to *TV Guide*.

> Turn off the gas and electricity. Leave a night-light to scare off intruders.

> Leave a note for the milkman. If you don't have a milkman, leave a note for your anaesthetist.

> Visit your therapist. If you don't have a therapist, call your mother.

> Leave a new message on your answering machine, like, "Owing to Doomsday, I will not be in for the rest of the afternoon."

7. Is it tacky to have a party the day before the world ends?

It depends on your personality. If you're a naturally gloomy person or a stick-in-the mud, you will probably want to absent yourself from felicity. No one likes a party pooper, so just stay home and listen to the "Missa Solemnis" and brood about how things got so goddamn depressing.

If, however, you are naturally ebullient and see the end of the world as a lark equivalent to the end of college finals, a party might be just the thing to help you get over the Armageddon blahs. You don't have to overdo it, it doesn't have to be as wild as the last days in Hitler's bunker, but certainly you could have some good friends over and break out a bottle of your best potassium cyanide. Put on a few records—"Bye-Bye, Love," "When Will I See You Again?", "It's All Over, Now" etc.—and play a few genteel party games.

Start a friendly betting pool predicting the exact moment the world will end. Or make a tontine, with everyone anteing up, and the last person surviving gets to keep the pot.

And who knows? If you've read this book carefully, the winner of that pot could be you.

After Doomsday, What?

"I think it's a fantastic adventure ahead, anticipating the collapse of civilization and riding through it, setting up a new system that will go on when you're gone."
—KURT SAXON, Survivalist author and publisher

Is this really *it?*

Well, you have to admit, things look pretty grim. Whoever invented doomsday knew what he was doing. When he said everybody goes, he meant *everybody*. No exceptions.

So—good-bye, everybody, it's been great knowing you. There, there, don't cry, it's not the end of the world. Oops! Actually, it *is* the end of the world, isn't it? What must I have been thinking? Well, you can't blame a man for being a little upset when . . .

Excuse me, someone is tugging on my sleeve and waving a book in my face. It's extremely inappropriate at a time like this to . . . I see. It's The Doomsday Book, and this joker has underlined something on page 75 that he wants me to read.

Hmm, interesting. Listen to this. It says that the good will be spared on Judgment Day.

Say, could it be? Have we found a loophole? Yes, it would appear that we have. It would appear that *some of us will be spared!* Hey, how about that!

Uh-oh, I just thought of something.

OK, so I haven't been a goddamn saint. So I blasphemed and fornicated a little. Sue me. But look, haven't I contributed to the Police Athletic League, the Salvation Army? Public Television? Didn't I send Aunt Mildred fifty bucks when she broke her hip? I've been *plenty* good, believe me, a lot better than some people sitting in this room, if you know who I mean.

Now that there is a distinct possibility that some of us will survive the apocalypse, we must begin looking beyond the system that brought us to this tragic pass and consider a new means of distributing capital, goods, and services. What's that, you say? You can't consider a new means of distributing capital, goods, and services until they pull you out from under the rubble? Well, we'll just start without you, and you can read the minutes.

The fatal flaw in the old capitalist system is that it was based on a very pessimistic view of human nature. It assumed that everybody is selfish, that people would prefer to accumulate money for themselves before considering the needs of other people. No wonder things got screwed up! But now that we have gotten rid of all those selfish people and created a brave new world where only the good exist, we can build some financial institutions on a foundation of love and benevolence, with goods and services distributed according to people's needs. As long as no one contemplates confiscating the hundred million I've already accumulated, I think the new system sounds dandy. I don't even mind your calling it Communism, just keep away from my safe.

As practically the entire human race will have been wiped out, the financial institutions of tomorrow will have to be considerably scaled down. The mighty banks of predoomsday times will be amalgamated into one building on the site of the old Mr. Milton's Beauty Salon. The new banks, disavowing the kind of business that got the old banks into such deep trouble, will be restricted from lending more than one cup of sugar to a customer on any given business day. The stock exchange, now headquartered in the pet food aisle of the old Grand Union, will utilize an entirely new approach to the measurement of capital gains, the Dow Schwartz Four Leading Cottage Industries Average. The commodities exchange will now be located where the Tenth Avenue Flea Market used to be (the exchange of fleas will play a significant role in the economic activity of the coming times). Naturally, the scale of business in the postapocalyptic era will be considerably more modest than what it used to be, but then you're only talking about ten or fifteen people left on earth, aren't you? I mean, you don't exactly need the World Trade Center for that kind of business, do you?

What will we do for currency? Clearly, old currencies like dollars and yen and pounds will no longer do, as they will have been debased to an infinitesimal fraction of their former value. There is already evidence that the U.S. government is mixing Hamburger Helper into its fifty-cent pieces. I'd like to recommend we start with a real humble currency, like pressed sawdust sandwiched between layers of formica. Red chips can be worth ten cents, blue ones a quarter, and imitation butcher block a dollar. That way, if there's an occasional panic, no one will get too badly burned.

It is not the form of currency that should concern us so much as the standard of exchange on which that currency rests. In the course of human history, that standard has always been precious metals, particularly gold. But look where the accumulation of gold has gotten us!

The postapocalyptic era will be founded on a new commodity which does not fluctuate wildly in value from day to day; something that has intrinsic desirability but not so much so that men lose their wits over it, as they did over gold; something universally acknowledged to have worth for people of all races, creeds, sexes, and places of national origin. Do I have something in mind? You're goddamn right I do. I'm thinking about mayonnaise. Mayonnaise as a standard of currency to replace gold? Don't scoff. They laughed at Pavlov when he invented dogs. The Mayonnaise Standard is an idea whose time has come, as any reader will agree after considering the following facts.

According to the University of Wisconsin's Russian, Italian, and Thousand Island Dressing Institute, at any given moment of the day human beings are spreading some five million metric tons of mayonnaise on sandwiches; folding it into chicken, tuna, or macaroni salads; or using it in a breathtaking variety of nonculinary applications such as industrial lubricants, bookbinding adhesives, and weather-resistant coatings for retired naval vessels. A day's consumption of mayonnaise spread over the city of Paducah, Kentucky, would cover everything but Fogelman's Department Store Annex; two days' worth, and you've got the Fogelman annex, too.

Mayonnaise is truly the Universal Spread. Yet we know more about the behavior of subatomic particles in a bubble chamber than we do about this homely concoction of egg yolks, vinegar, oil, and spices. Indeed, we know more, even, about ketchup than we do about mayonnaise. We know that ketchup will separate in a five-knot southerly breeze in the Horse Latitudes; or will, when mixed with kerosene, keep a garden party totally free of midges for up to eight hours; or, substituted for transmission fluid in the universal joint of an automobile, will cut slippage on a sharp curve by 20 percent. Yet we haven't the faintest idea why a shmear of mayo will exalt a pedestrian ham-and-American-on-white-down-hold-the-tommie to empyrean gustatory heights.

In the glorious heyday of Imperial Rome, mayonnaise flowed as freely as the waters of the Caracallan Baths, but the depredations of the barbarian hordes ended this custom as it did so many others. The sour, tart taste of mayonnaise was distinctly alien to the outlandish tongue (the Visigoths called it "Feh-Salsen"), and, had not an obscure order of Christian friars, the Bombazines, rescued the formula (one of history's minor ironies is that they used it not as a food but as *gesso* for their chapel frescoes), it would be as lost to us as the recipe for goat-lip turnovers, about which we know anything at all only from that tantalizing reference in Catullus.

With the exception of the *Verbosa Farrago Mayonnensis* of Fra Visus Lugubrius (who may justly be called the Patron Saint of Mayonnaise), not a single mention of the sauce is to be found anywhere in medieval literature. It is as if some gigantic Handi-wipe simply expunged it from the kitchen counter of history. Then, suddenly and dramatically, it shows up—where else?—in the notes and sketches of that restless genius Leonardo da Vinci. On page 189 (actually 981, since Leonardo wrote everything backwards) of his *Random Musings of a Renaissance Man,* we find an ink sketch of a modified siege weapon in which a gigantic ladle held taut by stretched cables is poised to chuck an immense blob of hot, rancid mayonnaise over the ramparts of a fortress. Beneath the drawing of this "Mayoballista," in Leonardo's exquisite mirror handwriting is the caption, "ratroM yrutneC hteitnewT fo rennureroF."

Subsequently, mayonnaise underwent what might be termed an identity crisis. People of the sixteenth, seventeenth, and early eighteenth centuries knew they had something here, but they weren't exactly sure what it was. Seventeenth-century scientists discovered pharmaceutical properties in it. Paramedicus declared it an excellent danderetic, pooperific, and grepsifacient. Muttle Ben-Galutzin, the illustrious Spanish rabbi, physician, and whale flenser, claimed to have utilized mayonnaise to good effect as a remedy for megrims, herpes (both zoster and simplex), flux, gripes, quinsy, dropsy, strismus, tabes, clonus, slough, blain, morbus gallicus, tic douloureaux, and heartburn.

Mayonnaise began to come into its own again late in the eighteenth century, but still not as a food. With the discovery by the Flemish chemist Haasel van der Zoom that mayonnaise heated to incandescence releases 6-diphynyl-ribosputin-asparagin-ashkenaze, a long-chain molecule which attacks the thoracic periphrasis of cockroaches, paralyzes their palps and knocks their spiracles into next Sunday, hot vaporized mayonnaise was used as a vermifuge in prisons, ships of the line, and bed-and-breakfasts all over England and the Continent.

Mayonnaise might, to this day, still be nothing more than an alternative to Flit, Raid, and Black Flag had not Pierre Nez de Canard, chef to Richard Wood-Tickinham, sixth Duke of Mayo, not inadvertently slopped some "vermifuge" into His Grace's tunny while shpritzing a large silverfish in the pantry. Mayo mistook the creamy blob for *sauce béarnaise* (though what he was doing putting *sauce béarnaise* on his tunny in the first place remains a mystery) and flipped a morsel of fish into his mouth. Mayo's guests gaped in wonder as a look of sheer ecstasy came over His Grace's face, and modern mayo as we know it had taken its place in the gastronomic pantheon of modern man (and woman, and woman, all right?).

Today, mayonnaise graces some of the most sublime recipes in the *maître de cuisine*'s repertoire, including *purée de poulet distrait, deshabille des canailles espagnoles, perigord aux borgogne lyonnaise,* and the indescribable *jambon du morgue.* Jacques Spratte, head chef of New York City's Le Mistrial and consultant to the Mayo Clinic, boasts that he uses at least a smidgeon of mayonnaise in every single dish he prepares—hence his nickname, "Mayo Jack." "There is no dish but cannot benefit from at least a soupçon of mayonnaise," the doughty little Gascon likes to say. "Mayonnaise is my trademark." Purists dispute him, and, indeed, some howl with outrage as Craig Claiborne did when he found his *pêche melba* swimming in it.

Aside from its alluring savor, mayonnaise is one of the most nutritious foods known to mankind. A single tablespoon of it contains a month's minimum requirements of otose, jocose, protean, casserine, cyanamid, leasco, gennesco, and zeppo. One could easily exist on nothing but mayonnaise, as, indeed, was the case of Shoji Yakinori, the Japanese soldier who recently emerged from a Kyoto bomb shelter seventy-five years after taking cover there at the outbreak of the Russo-Japanese war in 1904. Yakinori attributed his survival and excellent condition (he'd only lost one buttock) to the vast stores of mayonnaise on which he'd dined exclusively. His distinctive odor of piccalilli has provided scientists with a clue to mayonnaise's efficacy as a preservant.

Mayonnaise also has agricultural value. For centuries, Louisianans have used it to attract night crawlers before catfishing expeditions, and Texans spray it on pecan crops to promote "pie-ability" and discourage theft (it is impossible to climb a pecan tree covered with mayonnaise). A Virginia farmer who turned in exasperation to mayonnaise during the recent fertilizer pinch found his litchi yield doubled, his goobers sprouting in bumper volume, and pawpaws "big as brood mares."

Dismayingly, only thirteen scientific papers on the biomedical aspects of mayonnaise have been published in this century. The paucity of information on the subject is underscored by the fact that, in the same period, over 67,000 papers were published on penicillin, 33,000 on cortisone, and even 1200 on braunschweiger, for crying out loud! Yet people who have never cracked a scientific paper in their lives utilize mayonnaise as an antidepressant, a blood coagulant, an eyewash, an athlete's foot remedy, and a preparation for hemorrhoids. It makes suture scars disappear in half the time it takes the standard treatment, prevents itching in plaster casts, and reduces the heartbreak of psoriasis to a mere wistful throb.

Because of the paucity of hard data, the true biomedical value of mayonnaise is yet to be determined. One promising scientific experiment conducted by M.I.T. researchers does point the way, however. They grew staphylococcus bacteria in a culture of mayonnaise, and in a placebo culture of Durkee's Dressing, for fifteen weeks. At the end of this period, the Durkee's had turned a hideous jaundice yellow and smelled like Rockaway Channel at low tide. The mayo, on the other hand, was still white and creamy and indistinguishable from the original sample. However, when the mayonnaise was injected into the bone marrow of a rhesus monkey, greenish smoke roiled out of its ears, and within fifteen convulsive seconds its fles had assumed the consistency of a new place-kicking shoe.

Is it any wonder, then, that mayonnaise is gaining support with each passing day for its use as a new monetary standard to replace the no-longer reliable gold one? How difficult would it be to change the printing plates at the Treasury to replace "E pluribus unum" with "E gustibus mayo," or "In God we trust" with "For mayo we lust"?

Mayonnaise is indeed the Universal Spread, and because it is edible unlike gold, it brings a feeling of contentment to the user quite unlike the restless greed that possesses the gold bug. Perhaps conversion to the Mayonnaise standard will bring harmony, peace, and contentment to a human race that has never known it, obsessed as it has been with the acquisition and accumulation of riches and the concomitant vices of sexual lust and military belligerence with a side order of cheating at poker. I am counting on mayonnaise to do just that. Counting quite heavily, in fact, as you may have gathered from my recent purchase of five million tons of egg yolks, oil, vinegar, and spices, and a mayonnaise production facility in Biloxi, Mississippi.

So bring on your goddamn apocalypse; I'm ready for it!